The

SALESMAN

of the CENTURY

The

SALESMAN

of the CENTURY

Inventing, Marketing,
and Selling on TV:
How I Did It and
How You Can Too!

RON POPEIL

with Jefferson Graham

Delacorte  Press

Published by
Delacorte Press
Bantam Doubleday Dell Publishing Group, Inc.
1540 Broadway
New York, New York 10036

Library of Congress Cataloging in Publication Data
Popeil, Ron.
    The salesman of the century : Inventing, Marketing, and Selling on TV: How I Did It and How You Can Too! / Ron Popeil, with Jefferson Graham.
        p.   cm.
        ISBN 0-385-31378-0
        1. Popeil, Ron.   2. Businessmen—United States—Biography.
    3. Success in business—United States.   4. Inventions—United
    States—Marketing.   5. New products—United States—Marketing.
    6. Television advertising—United States.   7. Teleshopping—United
    States.   I. Graham, Jefferson.   II. Title.
    HC102.5.P66A3   1995
    658.8'4—dc20   95-3043
                                                                        CIP

Manufactured in the United States of America
Published simultaneously in Canada

November 1995

10   9   8   7   6   5   4   3   2   1

BVG

Contents

CONTENTS

Acknowledgments

This has been fun. It has been reflective and it has been a lot of hard work. I want to thank my editors Steve Ross and Jeanne Cavelos; the greatest sales-people I've ever encountered: Bob Bowersox, Steve Bryant, and Kathy Levine from QVC; my great friend Mel Korey; and especially Jan Gildersleeve, who had faith in me that I could write a book!

Ron Popeil

"I pushed. I yelled. I hawked. And it worked. I was stuffing money into my pockets, more money than I had ever seen in my life. I didn't have to be poor the rest of my life. Through sales I could escape from the poverty and the miserable existence I had with my grandparents."

Preface

You and I have never met, but in a way, we really have. I have been talking to you for over forty years through the TV set. I'm the guy who came on TV, usually late at night, to sell you a Veg-O-Matic, a Popeil Pocket Fisherman, or Mr. Microphone.

I'm Ron Popeil. As seen on TV. I'm an inventor and marketer of consumer products. I began selling at state and county fairs in the 1950s, beginning with products like the Chop-O-Matic that were made by my father, Sam Popeil. We found success together. Not that he couldn't have been successful without me. But I helped promote his products, not only by buying them from him (at a substantial profit) but also by selling them in such high volume. Once people saw how easy it was to sell his products, he got lots of new customers.

Over the years I invented my own products as well. TV classics like the Smokeless Ashtray, CleanAire Machine, Mr. Microphone, the Ronco Electric Food Dehydrator, and the

Popeil Automatic Pasta Maker. I've been in business over forty years and my company, Ronco, has sold over $1 billion worth of merchandise at retail.

One thing I've learned over the years is that the amount of ideas people have is unfathomable. Everyone's got at least one concept they think is clever, one they think is worth a million dollars. And they don't know what to do with it, so most of the concepts just remain ideas and don't go anywhere.

People come up to me all the time and say, "Ron, how can I become successful like you?" With this book I want to address all of the inventors, innovators, and future marketers out there, tell how I did it, show the steps to take, and hopefully help everyone avoid some of the expensive mistakes I've made.

I have the innate ability to come across products or ideas that will be well received by consumers. That's what separates me from everyone else. I'm the kind of individual who, if I believe in something, will focus on it, make sure it's done right, and lets the chips fall where they may. I believe I can share some of that wisdom with you and help you figure out what kind of products to market.

At the time we made the infomercial (a half-hour commercial) for the Ronco Electric Food Dehydrator in 1989, I had just come out of semiretirement. This was my comeback of sorts, and we opened the program by highlighting some of my past successes. Being in a reflective mood at the time, I felt I had been so successful that I wanted to use some of the infomercial time by giving back a bit to my customers. So in the middle of the infomercial show I announced that I would assist viewers by responding to their letters on inventions and marketing at no charge.

Those ten seconds of air time turned into a nightmare for me. I was inundated with thousands of letters from people who had an idea, but no clue about what to do or where to go. And I was really surprised that there were so many people out there seeking guidance.

I had to put together a team of people just to deal with all the mail and develop a form letter to cover most of the basic categories. Because I had a business to run, I couldn't just sit down and read every letter from every individual and then write back, because every product and situation is different.

Along with the letters, which took me away from what I do best—the creation of new products—some of the viewers even found my home telephone number, and I ended up spending a great deal of time on the phone trying to assist them.

Most would say, "Ron, I have a great product, but I can't tell you what it is." I would reply, "Don't tell me what your product is, tell me what your product does and we can work from there."

Later in the book I'll discuss how knowing what a product does is the most important component of marketing, as well as how to proceed from there. What to do about patents, product testing, prototypes, how to market a product using infomercials, home shopping channels, and retail. And hopefully, how you can make millions from your products like I have with mine. All it takes is the patience to build your empire slowly.

Every year I'm asked to speak at universities and seminars. I've been told by officials at UCLA, where I've lectured on direct marketing, that I'm one of their most sought-after speakers. Not too bad for a college dropout. While I regret that I didn't pursue my education (I can only think of how much more successful I would have become), I did gain very vital knowledge with true-life experience, and it's paid off handsomely. I'm a millionaire several times over and have several beautiful homes (despite what *People* said, I don't have a twenty-five-bedroom mansion. The last time I looked, it was just four! I'd love to know where the other twenty-one bedrooms are hidden).

Most people don't understand the nitty-gritty details behind products and the advertising that goes into making them successful. But it sure does look easy. Find a product, make an infomercial, put it on TV, and *voilà,* you are an instant multimillionaire.

In reality, it's a very difficult business, loaded with all sorts of problems. We'll discuss those problems and how to avoid them in Part 2 of this book, "Inventing and Marketing."

People often say to me, "Ron, how could you invent a Mr. Microphone and a Popeil Automatic Pasta Maker? They're so far apart." The answer is simple. I've always tried to look for needs in the marketplace. The formulas that I use work in any category.

Marketing is where it all begins. If you invent a great product and it hasn't been marketed properly, you'll never know whether the problem was with the invention or the marketing. Additionally, if you have a feeling for marketing, you not only can take your inventions to the marketplace and make them successful but you can also bring other inventors' products as well, which is what I've done over the years.

If you're capable of inventing only one or two products in your lifetime, just think about all the other products that are out there made by other people that you have access to because of your expertise in marketing.

The important thing is doing it. How many people do you know who have said over the years, "I have this great idea," but ten or twenty years later, it's still a great idea? Except in many cases, someone else took the initiative, did it, and now they're making all that money and you can end up saying to your friends and your relatives, "They took my idea!"

My philosophy is when you snooze, you lose. If you have a great idea, at least take the chance.

So please join me in *The Salesman of the Century.* As you turn the pages, we'll begin with the story of my life, about a guy who started with absolutely nothing and fulfilled the American Dream by selling his way to the top. Then we'll move on to inventing and marketing products, how to participate in the home shopping revolution, and go down memory lane a bit to discuss the beginnings of some of the greatest products from the Ronco gallery, including Veg-O-Matic, the Popeil Pocket Fisherman, Mr. Microphone, and the Buttoneer.

PART I

Bio

CHAPTER **1**

The Early Years

My childhood is a blur. I recall very little about it. Most of
the early years were so painful that I blocked much of it out.
I can tell you that I was born on May 3, 1935, in The Bronx,
the son of Julia and Samuel J. Popeil. My parents divorced
when I was three years old. Neither of them wanted me or
my older brother Jerry, so they dumped us and sent us off to
a boarding school in upstate New York. Instead of having us
adopted or something like that, they just got rid of the re-
sponsibility of parenting by shuffling us off to the school,
and later to our grandparents, my dad's parents. We were a
liability they chose not to accept.

I was in that school all year round from ages three to
eight along with my brother, who was seventeen months
older. Our parents never came to visit—not even at Christmas or New Year's.

I have one very vivid and painful memory from boarding
school. I remember one weekend when all the parents came
to visit their children. I hoped for a miracle, some sign of my

parents. I stood looking in the middle of this straight road that seemed to go on for an eternity, hoping to see a speck of a car coming in my direction, thinking that my family would come to visit us, but they never did. When I look back at my early years, this is my most vivid memory of boarding school. Just sitting on the road, crying, waiting for my mother and father to show up.

My brother Jerry was quite different from me. We didn't look alike, and we certainly didn't act alike. Jerry never took life very seriously. He had a very happy-go-lucky attitude and made a joke out of everything. I later discovered that we were half brothers. He was not my father's son. This information I picked up from my grandfather, who always delighted in saying that my mother was a tramp.

Jerry and I bunked together at boarding school, and when I was eight, my grandparents suddenly showed up one day, unannounced, and brought Jerry and me to Miami to live with them. They never explained to us why our parents had stuck us in boarding school for five years, or why we were going to live with them. We just went. The only time our parents were mentioned, they would knock my mother, side with their son, and blame her for the breakup of their marriage.

As with boarding school, I have blocked almost all the memories of my miserable life with my grandparents. They had a terrible relationship and fought all the time. In those days it seems (with the exception of my parents) that if you wed, you were married for life—good, bad, or indifferent. Both of them were miserable and did absolutely nothing about separating themselves from their suffering.

My father was a manufacturer of kitchen products, based in Chicago. He was now single, and lived in a hotel. His marital status was the reason why we didn't live with him, we were told. He had a business to run. We needed a family. Either way, he never visited us.

I don't remember who my grandfather worked for when we were in Florida. I don't remember him even having a job. We lived very frugally and ate peasant dishes most of the time—chicken feet, bean soups, and things like that. My grandmother was the kind of woman who would take advantage of coupons and sales, and walk miles to save fifty cents. I always told her that she was spending money to save money. What she saved she spent in wear and tear on shoe leather plus time, but to her, a bargain was a bargain.

My grandfather Isadore was a mean, unhappy man who didn't believe in anybody or anything. He was an immigrant from Poland and he graduated from the school of hard knocks. I don't think he ever told a joke—or laughed at one—in his life. I never called him Grandpa, Granddad, Izzy, or Isadore. In fact, I didn't call him anything. He never had a name as far as I was concerned.

My grandmother Mary, on the other hand, was a wonderful woman who never raised her voice. She spent most of her time in the kitchen cooking, and what I do remember fondly is hanging out in the kitchen and watching her cook. That, I believe, helps explain how I became fascinated with kitchen products. I learned how to cut onions and how to get into the nitty-gritty of vegetables and fruits. I learned how to pick them and what sizes and shapes to look for. I also learned many different recipes—Hungarian, Chinese, and a lot of heavy European dishes, all from my grandmother. When I look back, if there's any good that came out of the family, it originated with Grandma.

As a boy, I really wanted to have a dog, but my grandfather wouldn't let me. One day I found a lost dog who didn't have a home and begged my grandfather to let me keep him, but no dice. I was so starved for love, I thought having the pooch would improve my life. But like most things in his world, it was always negative. "No, you can't have the dog." Maybe that's why I have three dogs today.

Back then, I never daydreamed about things getting better one day. I think I was too young to analyze. I just went from one bad spot to another, which is why I think most of my childhood is blocked out. In fact, I don't even recall ever having a birthday party as a child.

We moved to Chicago when I was thirteen, and my grandfather was hired to run my father's factory. At the time, my father made products like the Spiral Slicer and the Slice-A-Way. The Spiral Slicer was a kitchen gadget with a little screw on the end. You would spin it around and get a potato that looked like it was a necklace. You could also make cottage fries. You see similar items on TV today utilized by other people as ancillary products to their main product. The Slice-A-Way was an early version of the Dial-O-Matic food slicer that I currently give away with the Ronco Electric Food Dehydrator. Back then most of my father's business was done via live demonstrations at county and state fairs and at dime stores like Woolworth's. His real success wouldn't come into play until television.

The first time I saw my father in many, many years was when we moved to the Windy City, but he was still very distant. Our other relative in Chicago was Uncle Raymond, my father's brother and business partner.

In Chicago we worked weekends with our grandmother and her husband at the cold, dark, and dingy Popeil Brothers factory. After five days of school, having to work on the weekends wasn't something we looked forward to. We wanted to play. We didn't even get paid for the work. I didn't even get a chance to see my father there because it was the weekend. He was never there on the weekends.

When I was sixteen, I discovered a whole new world, a place where I could break away from my bleak childhood. This new paradise was Chicago's Maxwell Street. The equivalent of a flea market today, it was a filthy, smelly street in a bad neighborhood, where people sold clothes, kitchen products, food, and knickknacks.

Maxwell Street was a Chicago tourist attraction, as well as a place to sell goods—some of them stolen goods. Thieves would go there to get rid of their hubcaps, steering wheels, radios, and other stuff. The first time I went there the proverbial light bulb went on over my head. I saw all these people selling product, pocketing money, making sales, and my mind went racing.

I can do what they're doing, I thought. *But I can do it better than they can.*

So I gathered up some kitchen products from my father's factory (he sold them to me at wholesale, so he made a full profit), and went down on a Sunday to give it a try. I pushed. I yelled. I hawked. And it worked. I was stuffing money into my pockets, more money than I had ever seen in my life. I didn't have to be poor the rest of my life. Through sales I could escape from poverty and the miserable existence I had with my grandparents. I had lived for sixteen years in homes without love, and now I had finally found a form of affection, and a human connection, through sales.

My uncle and dad—who had experience as demonstrators—didn't show me any tips on Maxwell Street. I picked up some of it by watching others, but mostly I just learned on my own. I went out every weekend, selling everything from kitchen gadgets to shoeshine spray.

I would arrive at five A.M., put my table together, make sure my portable microphone worked (I hadn't invented Mr. Microphone yet), and start cutting up the food. If I sold a food chopper, for instance, I would have bowls on the counter with nice vegetables in different colors—peppers, onions, cabbages, et cetera. It was nothing for me to cut up, say, fifty pounds each of onions, cabbages, carrots, and a hundred pounds of potatoes in a day.

Make no mistake: this was very hard work. In the summer it was really hot, and in the winter it was freezing. The tables I used were housed at a fish store, and you know what that could smell like. While my peers were off going to the movies and the malt shop, I was making money on this dirty, filthy, smelly street.

I hated going there. But when I spent the money I made there, nobody said, "Where did this money come from? Is this money coming from you being a lawyer or a doctor, or some credible profession like that?" Nobody ever asks you where the money comes from. They just take it. Money is money. It all looks the same when you're spending it.

Financially it was well worth it. Here I was, sixteen years old, a high school kid who was making what seemed like a fortune on Maxwell Street. Sometimes I worked both Saturday and Sunday, grossing $500 a day, which was great pay for anyone in the 1950s. In fact, it wouldn't be too bad for a kid in the 1990s either. Setting up the stand was a pain. Standing on Coca-Cola boxes in one place without moving was also very hard on my legs and feet. And because I had to talk loudly from six A.M. to four P.M. my voice at the end of the day was strained and hoarse. But selling came easy for me. And it was very satisfying. Selling on Maxwell Street was security. Making money was survival.

I hadn't yet decided what to do with my life. I didn't enjoy school and had trouble achieving the kinds of grades other students were getting. How could I care about school with the kind of money I was reaping on Maxwell Street?

Selling just seemed to come naturally to me. I found that I could instantly discover the hot buttons of a product; the magic words that would make someone think they needed to part with their cash. At that stage of my life I felt like I could sell anything. Even if my family didn't teach me about demonstrating, I still came from a family of men who sold products at fairs and stores. Something must have been in my genes. And after all of those years of distant relations I was determined to prove that I could be the greatest salesman of them all.

CHAPTER 2

Woolworth's

I moved out of my grandparents' house when I was seventeen. The exit was provoked by a big fight with my grandfather. Living with him had become unbearable. We had an argument over something minor and he slapped me in the face. I looked him in the eye and said sternly, "If you ever raise your hand to me again, I'll knock your block off." I vowed he would never hit me again without a response. And I moved out.

I got my own studio apartment in Chicago and spent more time on Maxwell Street and at other fairs and shows. I went to the University of Illinois for a year, but with the money I was making as a street vendor, I just couldn't get into schoolwork and quit.

My really big break in life was getting a job at the Woolworth's at State and Washington streets in Chicago. This wasn't just any Woolworth's, but the top-grossing Woolworth store in the country. The manager of the store, Rick Edel, was the highest-paid manager in the Woolworth chain.

He told me that he received a perk no other Woolworth's manager could claim: a commission on total profits.

Mr. Edel was different from the other Woolworth's managers in the chain. Always impeccably dressed, he looked and carried himself like a big-city politician. He was even driven to work every day in a limousine by one of the store employees. Celebrities used to come in all the time to meet him and pose for pictures. He was like the Mayor Daley of State Street.

It used to drive the corporate people who ran Woolworth's crazy that they had a manager who lived better than they did. There was nothing they could do—the store was the most profitable in the chain. And Mr. Edel used to get a big kick out of taking guests and dignitaries up on the second-floor balcony, where you could look out at the entire first floor, and point down to me. "See that kid down there?" he would say. "He makes more money than I do!"

This was true, because I had cut a great deal with him: If the store didn't make any money, they weren't out a dime. Woolworth's didn't pay me a salary, but instead they took 20 percent of the total dollars I brought in. I purchased the product myself (mostly my dad's gadgets and other products of that type—food choppers, shoeshine spray, plastic plant kits), sold them, and put the money in the cash register. At the end of the week the store took its cut and gave me a check for the balance. And since I was an independent contractor, I had the freedom to leave Woolworth's during the summer to work the fair circuit. I was raking in $1,000 *a week* for myself at a time when the average *monthly* salary was about $500.

The dimestore was the Wal-Mart or Kmart of its day. Where America shopped. They were perfect arenas for demonstrating because of the heavy foot traffic. The consumer would walk into the store with no intention of buying your product, and I had to stop them, create the desire, and make them walk away with it.

Woolworth's No. 1 was L-shaped in design, your typical Woolworth's store, with a cafeteria upstairs, the main level, and the basement. My stand was always in a good location on the State Street side of the store near the main entrance. No sooner had you walked into the store than you were confronted with my voice, my crowd, and my demonstration.

I always liked to choose my own location. Getting a good location for demonstrating at Woolworth's isn't any different from getting a prime location at a county fair. Why would anyone want to be in the basement, where there's no serious traffic? What I learned at Woolworth's was that cosmetics always yielded the highest traffic, with women coming in to buy lipstick, combs, eye shadow, and other similar products. So that's where I stood, all day long, next to cosmetics. At county and state fairs, the best location was normally near the ladies' washroom.

Mel Korey, a friend I met at the University of Illinois, came down to Woolworth's one day to meet me for lunch. Listen to him describe the scene:

"Ron had been my friend and roommate, but I'd never seen him work. I wasn't prepared and didn't know what to expect. I'd seen demonstrators in stores before; they'd have a few people in front of them, and maybe a sale or two or three. Big deal. But Ron made it an art form.

"I walked in the State Street entrance and the first thing I noticed in the massive store was a huge crowd of people about thirty yards ahead. It was Ron giving a demonstration. Ron had changed since I had last seen him at school. His hair had a different style, his features had chiseled, and with his blue-green eyes and white teeth he seemed like a younger version of Paul Newman—or at least that's what the ladies seemed to think.

"He used his looks as he played the crowd. Each five- to

ten-minute sales pitch would be slightly altered to the makeup of his audience, and each seemed completely ad-libbed. I noticed secretaries and office people who would spend their entire lunch breaks eating while watching continuous demonstrations as the sales kept multiplying and the money rolled in.

"At the end of the day we finally had time to visit. Ron gave me his hand to shake. His hand and forearm were like steel. That came from doing multiple demonstrations all day, six days a week."

When we sell product on live demonstration, we make people go down into their purses or pockets and take out money for a product they had had no intention of buying. Experience taught me that when selling to a crowd, the hardest person to sell was always the guy smoking a pipe. But then, I knew that if I could sell that pipe smoker, everybody else would be duck soup. If I ever had people in my audience who smoked pipes, I would focus directly on them. They are the hardest people to sell because they don't make quick decisions. They're very methodical in their thinking and do everything slowly. They're much slower to reach down into their pockets. So if you can sell them, you can hook the entire crowd.

Another live demonstration technique is focusing on the people who you feel are the most interested. The ones who nod as you speak. If you can get them to buy, the others will follow. A lot of people only buy because other people are buying the product. They don't want to miss out on the action.

For instance, my cousin Archie, who sold knickknacks on the boardwalk in Atlantic City back in the 1950s, once found a guy in his crowd who couldn't stop buying all of his products. Every time Archie brought out a new item, the guy bought. Later, when my cousin took a break from selling, he

saw his great customer walk away with two full shopping
bags. He stopped, looked into both shopping bags, paused,
then walked over to a garbage can. He threw both bags in
the can and walked away.

I think that says it all. He just got caught up in the rap-
ture of buying.

Working at Woolworth's was as exciting as it was exhaust-
ing. Every day, six days a week, for ten to twelve hours, I
stood there talking nonstop, voice cracking, hardly ever taking a break because that would mean lost business. I had a
friend at Woolworth's named O'Neil Jones who couldn't understand how I could stand there talking at a high pitch for
so many hours without stopping. He used to bring me water
to drink because he knew I wouldn't take the time for a
break or lunch. (Mel Korey and I both still help support
O'Neil Jones today. We've never forgotten his help and support.)

In the business of demonstrating, you're not just taking
cash from people. You're also keeping the momentum going.
Let's say you work a crowd and sell to fifty percent. Half
walk away, the other half buy the product. And you're making sales as fast as you can put money in a register. When you
get down to the last three or four sales, you wait before taking their money. You tell those people you have one more
thing you want to show them before you make the sale. And
that will be the nucleus or the beginning of the next audience. So when the next hundred people start to build, and
they're watching you demonstrate again, you make a slight
variation on your pitch for the four or five people you didn't
take the money from.

The crowd builds behind them and locks them in so they
couldn't leave even if they wanted to. And then when you tell
them the price of the product again, they're the ones who
take their money out and throw it at you instantly. Even be-

fore you mention the price, they have their money out, because now they've heard the sales pitch twice, and they're sold. They can't wait to have the product. The rest of the audience sees them going for their money, and now they want to buy the product too. They have to have it!

With momentum like that I couldn't just shut up and walk away. Had I done that, when I returned, I would have had to start from scratch all over again. With no one in front of me.

My raps at Woolworth's were all basically the same. I'd introduce the product and tell the customers why it could improve their life. *"You can take a knife and try to chop it this way or you can use the food chopper. You can crush ice for mixed drinks or snow cones for the kids. You can chop ham for ham salad, chicken for chicken salad, horse for horse radish."*

I would announce the suggested retail price and tell them about the special offer I was prepared to make. "For the first twenty people who reach down into their purse or pocket right now, I'm going to give you this kitchen utensil absolutely free." Then I would look out at the crowd and assign numbers—number one, number two, number three, and so on. At this point people couldn't wait to get into their pockets to take out their money. They weren't even looking at the free product they were going to get with it. They didn't care. They just didn't want to be number twenty-one, the guy or gal who got left out. From time to time there would be a customer who stood there, who looked like they wanted to buy the product but didn't open up their purse or go down into their pockets to take out the money as the other people did. And when I said to them, "Aren't you going to get one?" the response would be, "You already passed out the twenty." I said, "Oh, I think you made a mistake. I don't think you heard me correctly. I said, the first twenty . . . *thousand.*"

And then they laughed, went into their pockets, and bought the product. (You never use the word *buy,* because that's a negative. In this situation I knew they were going to buy it. It's never good to ask a question, because you're going to get one of two answers, and no is usually the automatic response. You never want to pose the question. In telemarketing, when they do their upsell sales presentation, they say, "Can I add that to your order?" It is a question, but it's not confrontational.)

In a television infomercial, we currently don't have the luxury of interacting with our customers or being able to whip the audience into a frenzy to buy the product before someone else buys it. But the day is coming close with interactive TV.

One of my Woolworth's experiences has stuck with me all my life and influenced the naming of one of my most successful products. Remember GLH (Great Looking Hair) Formula #9, the "hair in a can"? You may think I call it Formula #9 because I tested nine different formulas until I came up with the best one. But this is not exactly the case.

Back in my Woolworth's days a man named Charlie Kasher invented a hair product called Charles Antel Formula #9 and was quite successful with it. He subsequently sold the product for $1 million to a company called Gulf American Land, Inc., whose basic business was real estate. Charlie took the million, and went into the movie production business, as one of the producers of the early James Bond movies.

I found this amazing. A guy comes out of a Woolworth's store selling hair products, and the next thing you know, he's in the movie business and making a fortune with Agent 007. So when I was thinking of a name for my first hair product, I naturally thought of Charlie and how well his Formula #9 served him.

•

When I moved out of my grandparents' house, my brother Jerry moved as well. He worked for me at Woolworth's and I helped him by teaching him how to demonstrate products. Jerry was a very funny guy who everybody liked. He wouldn't hurt a fly but he couldn't deal with authority. He was the original Forrest Gump.

At Woolworth's he would take over my stand when I went on vacation, or sometimes run another stand in the store, selling another product. I owned the goods and would give Jerry and the store a share of the gross sales.

Well, one day the manager of the store, Rick Edel, passed Jerry's stand as he was demonstrating. Rick overheard Jerry tell his customers at the end of his sales pitch when he was passing out the merchandise: "You want one and you want one, and the lady wants one in the rear. . . ." Was he talking about her ass or someone in the back row? Rick took the first meaning and he was furious. "Jerry," he said, "don't ever say that again. If you do, I'll throw you out of the store."

That was authority talking to Jerry, and as such, it went in one ear and out the other. Rick caught him saying it again, and this time he became even more furious. He threatened to ban Jerry from Woolworth's again. But that didn't stop my brother.

When Rick caught him saying those words a third time, on his way back from lunch, he simply exploded. He berated Jerry for what seemed like ten minutes and everybody in the store could hear every word. Remember that Woolworth's No. 1 was a big store with hundreds of employees and it covered almost an entire city block.

When Rick finally stopped, my brother just looked down at him and said, "Mr. Edel, you wouldn't be talking to me that way if you weren't drinking."

Jerry was later drafted by the Air Force. On his first day the sergeant called out the names of the new men and when he said, "Popeil," Jerry didn't answer. When the sergeant asked him why he didn't answer, he said, "Because you didn't say, 'Jerry Popeil.' "

In the military they like their men to be spick-and-span. Jerry's clothes were always wrinkled and messy. One day a colonel walked by him and said, "Young man, have your clothes cleaned and pressed. That's an order." The next day the colonel saw him and naturally Jerry hadn't cleaned up his act. And like Rick Edel the colonel gave Jerry one more chance. But when Jerry didn't respond to his threats, he didn't just scream—he threw Jerry in the brig, where he spent most of his time in the Air Force eating the cookies my grandmother sent him.

And what did I learn from my Woolworth's experience? The value of instant feedback and dealing with lots of people on a one-to-one level. Working in front of crowds, I instantly found out whether my retail price was too high or too low. Working at Woolworth's wasn't that much different from a home show or a fair. The same thing happens: You sell product to one person at a time and do your research and testing right on the spot. They ask the right questions that help sharpen your presentation.

CHAPTER 3

The Fair Circuit

Thanks to Woolworth's I was now well off. I wouldn't say I was rich, but considering where I had come from I certainly felt wealthy. My father, during one of those rare times when we had a conversation, said to me, "Be careful, Ron. The more money you make, the more money you'll spend." I assured him that it wouldn't happen to me.

But he was right and I was wrong. I started staying in $150- to $200-a-night hotel suites, dined at swanky restaurants (the original Pump Room in Chicago, a celebrity hangout, was my favorite), drove fancy cars, traveled to exotic places, and bought myself a beautiful shiny Rolex watch.

But living extravagantly wasn't enough. Sure, I was making great money at Woolworth's, but during the summers I also felt the need to put in a lot of long hours at the fairs, which was no picnic. In the Midwest summer days can be really hot and uncomfortable. At the end of the day, after talking nonstop for ten to twelve hours, I had no voice. But the money was great and thousands of people were there. You couldn't keep me away.

At the fairs I rarely worked outside. I liked to demonstrate in the buildings, playing it safe because of the weather. One thing that could kill you if you worked outside at a fair was rain. But if you were inside, people would run into the buildings for shelter. If the weather was nice, that could also work against you (because no one would come inside), but in the Midwest that didn't usually happen.

As far as the best location to sell at fairs, I didn't look for the lipstick stand like I did at Woolworth's, but instead another women's favorite—the bathroom. If you could sell near the ladies' bathroom you were always guaranteed one of the heaviest concentrations of foot traffic at the fair.

Inside the buildings people sold a lot of blenders, car waxes, spark intensifiers (for better gas mileage), vibrating chairs, mops, food choppers, and knives. The knives were really big because they didn't take up a lot of space, and guys could throw them in the back of a truck. The chairs were popular because when you walk around a fair all day, you get tired, and there's never anywhere to sit down. So the guy selling a vibrating chair always had more customers than he could handle.

Of the products sold at fairs during my era, it's interesting how many of them went on to become infomercial staples: amazing car waxes, blenders (aka juicers), knives (anyone ever heard of the Ginsu?), kitchen gadgets, gas additives, and mops.

After Mel Korey graduated from college, I asked him to join me on the fair circuit. I'd handle the expenses, and give him a commission of 25 percent on whatever he sold. Mel was a would-be musician. He liked to sing but jobs were few. He didn't know much about sales, but he was my friend and I welcomed the company.

County and state fairs and other shows (auto, flower, home and garden) run anywhere from two to twenty days. We usually began with the Illinois State Fair in Springfield, followed by the Wisconsin State Fair near Milwaukee, the Ohio State Fair in Columbus, the North Carolina State Fair in Raleigh, and the Eastern States Exposition in Springfield, Massachusetts.

We brought three products that summer. Two were made by my father: the Feather Touch Knife and the Kitchen Magician. Dad's dagger was what most people know today as the Ginsu, a serrated-edged knife that never needed sharpening. It would glide through the softest tomato, fresh baked bread (part of the demonstration), and even cut through a package of frozen food (the clincher!).

The Kitchen Magician was a simple gadget. The tip was a radish rose maker, then there was a peeler and grater, and when you turned it inside out, the inner unit could be used to serrate melons, fruits, and vegetables.

We also sold the Plastic Plant Kit, which consisted of tubes of liquid plastic in a variety of "leafy colors" along with an assortment of metal plates with inverted leaf designs, stems, and green tape. The consumer would run the liquid plastic along the border of the leaf, fill it in the mold, add a stem, and put it under a heat lamp or over a toaster. It dried quickly and they had a leaf. A bunch of leaves attached together made a complete plant.

In Springfield, in our separate booths, the plan was to demonstrate the Feather Touch Knife and Kitchen Magician. I coached Mel on his presentation, in what order to use the products on which vegetables and how to play the crowd and how to strengthen the "turn" (asking for the money).

We got to Springfield on a Thursday night and the next morning I called Mel to pick him up. At five A.M. he was a little surprised at the early wake-up call, as he wasn't used to getting up that early. But on the fair circuit that's when we began. We needed to get to the produce market and buy all the fruits and vegetables for the day. Then it was off to the fair to make the displays for the booths, which were open to the public at eight A.M. As with Maxwell Street, it wasn't simply a matter of showing up, demonstrating products, and raking in the bucks. We also had to prep the stands to make the display look appetizing—which took a lot of time—and peel tons of onions so we could slice or chop them up.

We sorted the tomatoes, lemons, melons, breads, and assorted vegetables and went to work at our respective booths. At two P.M., after I had made $350, I went over to Mel's booth to see how he was doing. I asked Mel how much money he had taken in. A grand total of $8. Mel had decided to quit. "Ron, I want to go home," he told me. "I don't know what I'm doing. I'm not cut out for this."

"Wait a minute," I said. "If you had to sing before this crowd, could you do it? If you had to play baseball or basketball here, couldn't you cut it?"

"Sure," said Mel, "because those are things I know I can do."

"You can do it," I said. "Don't ever give up. Be in control. Take command of yourself."

Mel went back to his booth and tried again. And he proceeded to pull in another $8.

Over dinner, I told him to forget working his booth in the morning. Instead, I wanted him just to watch me.

Mel's recollections of that morning:

"I watched Ron build up and work his audience. He made them like, accept, and believe him. I'd watch him make a radish rose (every time I tried to make one the damn petal fell off!). I'd watch him take a strip of lemon peel off a lemon, grate and peel a carrot, slice cucumbers paper thin, have a child from the audience use the knife to show how easy it was to use, 'glamorize' assorted fruits, and offer the first ten buyers a special price on the knife, along with the

Kitchen Magician for free. Then I'd watch fathers give two dollars and a nickel ($1.98 plus tax) to their wives and to each of their kids—"one set per family." This was simply too good an offer to pass up!"

Mel was ready to try again and some of my training began to pay off. He took in $150. The next day it was up to $200. Then $600. By the final day of the fair Mel got all the way up to $1,200. He was finally getting the art of fair salesmanship.

The fair circuit's demonstration area had its stars. A guy named Bob Eustace hawked a product that would clean glasses, mirrors, windshields, *and* prevent fogging. There was Harry Mathieson, from England, who sold a variety of food items. My favorite, probably the greatest pitchman ever, was Frenchy Bordeaux, who engaged in the fine art of the "jam auction." Frenchy's techniques taught me a lot about human nature and sales.

Frenchy would work off the back end of a truck, which was loaded with merchandise. The back of the truck was his stage. He would get an audience by simply saying into his microphone, "Who out there would like a free lighter?"

If you were passing by and you heard someone say that, you'd say, "Wait a minute. He's got to be kidding." But Frenchy would prove his seriousness by taking several handfuls of lighters and throwing them out in all directions. People would run to pick them up. And he would keep doing this until he had attracted a crowd.

"Who needs a pen?" he'd say, and now people knew this guy was for real. And he'd throw pens out. He's just tossed maybe twenty dollars worth of merchandise, and now the jam auction is ready to begin.

"I've got some items up here," he'd say, "but first I need to find out some information. I want to know who in my audience has faith in the auctioneer. I have this portable radio worth twenty dollars. . . ." He'd turn it on and play it into the microphone. A little tinny radio now would sound big and expensive coming out of the loudspeakers. "Who will give me a dollar for it?"

Hands are raised.

"I'm going to pass out fifty radios for a dollar, but I can only take fifty buyers. Who will give me a dollar for the radio?" More hands go up and he'd select fifty customers, by giving them each a number, one, two, three, and so on.

"Raise your hands if you have a number and hold up your dollar. Would you say a radio is a good auction buy for a dollar? What? I can't hear you."

At the world's roar of approval Frenchy takes the dollars, wraps them around the radios, hands both back to his customers, and then says to them, "What do you say?"

"Thank you."

He makes each one say thanks individually. One by one. He gets them to participate.

"That's what I wanted to hear."

Now he moves to a gold pen-and-pencil set, which he says has a retail value of $39.95, and he repeats the exercise, taking the dollars, and then giving them back with the free pens and pencils.

Now he's ready for his big score—a sewing machine, worth $600. "Who in my audience would pay $200 for this sewing machine? Would you think that was a good auction buy? If so, please raise your hands."

Some fifteen hands go up.

Frenchy ups the ante by throwing in a $69.95 watch (he calls it "Bordeaux Geneva") and collects another twenty customers.

Then he throws in some $30 pearl earrings. "Now you have a sewing machine, a watch, and pearl earrings. How many out there think that's a good auction value?"

By now, he has seventy customers ready to reach into

their pockets and fork over $200. He takes the money and then dashes off for a break. Of the $200, he had a cost factor of around 50 percent, so he made a profit of $100 per person. He sold seventy people and made $7,000 in forty-five minutes. Not bad for less than an hour's work. And he did this several times a day.

So what did Frenchy teach me? That people are always looking for value. True, what he was doing was a scam, but don't forget that people have never lost their taste for getting things free. People want to know they're getting a lot for their money. The word *free* is now associated with so many products sold on TV. Buy one, get one free. Buy this knife, and we'll throw in a set of steak knives too. Call now for the Popeil Pasta Machine, and I'll include a free Popeil Bagel Cutter and Knife too.

Frenchy conned people into buying product, but he didn't give them value. Today we've got the money-back guarantee. Back then, if you took the product home and weren't happy, what were you going to do—return it to the truck next year when the fair came back?

Working the fairs was a great learning experience for me because I was surrounded by the master salesmen of my field. At Woolworth's there might be one or two other demonstrators, but at the fairs there would be ten or fifteen, and I learned how to improve my sales techniques by watching their presentations.

CHAPTER **4**

The General

At Woolworth's one of my most successful products was the Instant Shine shoeshine spray. It was great because it was very easy to demonstrate, priced right, and there was lots of need for it. The product was good for children, who were always scuffing their shoes up, women, who drove in cars and got their heels dirty, and businessmen, for obvious reasons.

Instant Shine was a clear spray that came in an aerosol can and was designed to put a high-gloss shine on shoes. It could do any color shoe and was usually sold via demonstration. At Woolworth's I would make my presentation by stopping the customer in the store and shining one of their shoes very quickly. I would show off the difference between a nice shine from my spray, and their dull shoe on the other foot. I would tell the customer about the value of having such a product work in a minute or so. Then I would do the other shoe, tell 'em the price, and watch them pull out their money.

We sold Instant Shine on the fair circuit as well, where we

did great business with sales tactics like stopping passersby and yelling, "Free shoeshine!" or "Hey, nice shoes," and then dropping down to give them a shine. One of the best lines came from my brother Jerry, who lay on the ground and said, "Help me! Help me!" When the good Samaritan came over to help Jerry up, he would respond by shining one of their shoes and trying to make a sale. And he usually did!

We always did great with Instant Shine. It was clear there was a huge market here. So I brainstormed to see how we could make even more bucks. Always thinking about mass market, I asked myself a very important question: Who needs to have their shoes shined more than anyone else? The obvious answer: the military.

So I set out to make the greatest sale ever. I didn't know anyone in the Army, but I did discover the existence of an armory on the North side of Chicago, which was filled every Wednesday night with members of the National Guard. Through a connection I was able to get introduced to a Captain Carvelli and I offered him a small piece of the action if he could get me into the armory on Wednesdays to work the crowd.

So Mel Korey and I loaded up our cars and trunks with cases and cases of Instant Shine and came to the armory. There were hundreds of guys in the stadium, all under one roof. We walked in, and the sergeant introduced us.

"Attention," he said. "At ease, gentlemen. Mr. Ron Popeil is here with a product that's been authorized by the National Guard. It shines shoes. For you lazy guys out there who don't like shining your shoes and keeping them the way we want it, here's a product that will save you lots of time and energy." (He practically did the sale for us right there.)

I addressed the crowd, told the men about the benefits of Instant Shine, said it only cost $1.99, and that they could meet Mel and me in the office, where we would be happy to sell them as many cans of the spray as we had.

We sold tons. The guys in the National Guard wanted something that was fast and easy to shine their shoes and we had it for them.

Now on top of my weekly $1,000 from Woolworth's, I was pulling in an additional $500. For one night's work. Not bad. But still not good enough.

I had another idea. A few months later I met with Captain Carvelli and said, "Captain, you know we can go bigger than this."

"What do you want to do, Ron?"

"I want to sell the entire National Guard for the whole state of Illinois." I didn't just want one giant armory. I wanted the whole state. All over Chicago, all over the country, all over the world, armed forces troops wore boots. Boots that were *required* to be shined! Now, that's the true meaning of the words *mass market*.

The captain told me I would have to meet with the general.

I had never met a general before. The highest ranking officer I had ever met, even at the armory, was a captain. But we got in to meet with the general, thanks to Captain Carvelli.

It was a hot August summer night when we went to meet with the man. I packed up a couple cases of Instant Shine, and Mel and I knocked on his door. A sergeant opened it up, looking very threatening, much like a professional bodyguard. He wore a crisp shirt, his back was straight, and he was very, very serious.

The general's setup was the biggest office I had ever seen in my life. And I'll never forget the carpeting. The color was royal blue, and when I stepped on it, my foot seemed to sink down six inches. I had never stepped on carpeting that plush before.

The general was sitting at the end of his office behind a desk. He motioned to us to come in. There was one seat in front of the desk and the other was directly behind it. I sat in front with Mel behind me.

"How can we help you?" asked the general.

"Well, General, we've been selling the National Guard our shoeshine spray and it's worked successfully and we'd like to sell it to the entire National Guard for the state of Illinois. Let me show you how it works."

I didn't ask him if I could demonstrate the product on his shoes. I just grabbed a can out of the case and, without being invited, walked behind the general's desk and looked at his boots. I could see out of the corner of my eye that the sergeant was standing at the edge of his desk watching every move I made. He was glaring at me, and with good reason. When I looked at the general's boots they were so shiny, I could see my face in them. They certainly didn't need shining.

Still, I sprayed the first boot and made sure the sergeant could see the difference between my boot and the boot he had done. (The sergeant was assigned to the general. He was the one who had to keep the general's boots spit-shined.) Then I sprayed the other boot and kept talking to the general about the benefits of Instant Shine. About twenty seconds passed. Then I got a huge shock: the general's boots had turned snow white. As in the color of Ivory soap. His beautiful brown boots were now totally white. And so was my face.

Still, my mind started to work very quickly. I didn't know what to say so I tried this one: "That shine will come back again the way it was before." I just didn't know what year.

I thought there might be something wrong with the can, so I looked at Mel, but he had frozen to ice. His mouth was wide open, he was not blinking, and he appeared to be in a catatonic state. "Mel," I said, "would you go back and hand me that case over there, please?"

Mel found a way to get up, and handed me another case

of the spray. I gave it to the general, asked him to pick out any can he liked, and requested another pair of boots.

The general said, "Sergeant, get me another pair of boots." But the sergeant did not move. The general responded with another order. "I said get me another pair of boots!"

"Yes, sir," replied the sergeant, who went out and came back with another pair of stunning, beautiful, spit-shined boots.

I sprayed the second pair of boots, and they both looked great. For a second or two. Then, it happened again. These boots also turned snow white. So now the general was a proud owner of two pairs of white boots. The sergeant looked at me like I was a thief who had come to rob him. Mel had turned back to ice. One thing was very clear: We needed to get out of this office and never come back again. So I went for broke. I gathered all my nerve, looked the general in the eye, and said, "Well, General, can we sell the National Guard?"

He looked at me, then down at his boots, and paused.

"Well, if it's okay with Colonel Kane, it's okay with me."

And with that, Mel and I flew out of there, never to return.

Who was Colonel Kane? I didn't know then, but we learned later on that he was a highly connected military official. The general had thought we were associated with him in some way, and whatever the colonel wanted was fine with him—even if it did make boots turn white.

Now, the moral of the story?

How could I do what I did to the general's boots and then look the general in the eye and have the nerve to say what I did? When something is all lost, you might as well go for it. Don't just fall down and play dead. I think the ability to do something like that gives you some insight into a good salesperson. Not giving up. I could have apologized and said I was sorry and tried to figure out later what happened. But that wouldn't have created a sale. I never did follow up, for obvious reasons, but at least I left the window open.

As for why the boots turned white: We found out that high humidity caused a chemical reaction on the boots, something I had never experienced within the walls of Woolworth's. So I stopped selling Instant Shine, because I believe that you have to sell a quality product. I chose not to market it rather than hurt my reputation. We were on the verge of something big but the product let us down.

CHAPTER 5

Marriage and Family

I did so well at the Chicago Woolworth's that I decided it was time to move to New York City in 1956 and take on the Big Apple. I went to work at the big Woolworth's store on Thirty-fourth Street in Herald Square.

But life was not decidedly better in New York. In fact I hated New York. It was crude and dark. People used terrible language. I couldn't wait to get out of there.

So I did what many another homesick kid would do. I called a girl I dated occasionally, Marilyn, and asked her to marry me.

I wasn't in love. But for some reason I saw marriage as the perfect way to get out of New York and back to Chicago. I knew I didn't marry for the right reason.

I had met Marilyn during my year at the University of Illinois, where I got caught up in the pressures of the times. I was living at the fraternity dorm (rooming with Mel Korey). I dated Marilyn for a few months. Then I asked her to go steady with me, because that's what everyone was doing.

You dated a girl and then asked her to go steady. My frat brothers told me that after so many months you were supposed to "lovalier" her, then pin her. Well, I did that. And then the next step was engagement. And then marriage. I just followed what everyone else did.

Marilyn and I stayed together for seven years, and we had two beautiful children, Kathryn and Shannon. The relationship didn't work out because I was too busy doing my thing. She was a really good person. The marriage not working certainly wasn't her fault, but mine.

I married two other times. I don't know what this says about me and the Seven Year Itch, but all three marriages only lasted seven years each.

Shirley Dupre, an airline stewardess, was my second wife. I met her while working at Woolworth's in Chicago on a day when she was on her first flight for Delta Airlines. She was another terrific girl, but I screwed this one up too. She was a good wife, but I just wasn't a good husband.

Wife number three was Lisa Boehne of Orange County, California. We met at a party in Los Angeles, started seeing each other, and subsequently got married. The good news about this union is the wonderful child we had, Lauren. Twelve years old as this book goes to print, Lauren now spends about half her time with me and half her time with her mother. You've probably seen Lauren on my Food Dehydrator and Pasta Machine infomercials.

It's been such a joy to watch Lauren grow up, now that I have more time to enjoy the experience of parenting than I did back in the sixties and seventies. I also have to admit that I'm a much better father now than I was for Shannon and Kathryn. For them, on a scale of one to ten, I was probably a three.

I basically followed in the footsteps of my father, who wrapped himself totally in his work and paid no mind to his children. I'm very close with Kathryn and Shannon today and try to give them a lot of the love I should have given them in the past. But I feel embarrassed about the lost years. It's somewhat uncomfortable looking back and realizing that I unconsciously acted like my father. I did not make that mistake with Lauren.

I saw my mother only once in later life. At the time I was in my twenties and successful, and we had lunch in New York. She had remarried. I never asked her why she abandoned us. I had been told so many horrible things about her by my grandfather that I just didn't want to bring up any of those subjects. What would getting into it and making her feel bad accomplish?

We spent an hour together, I gave her some money because I thought she needed it and that was the last I saw of her. I never saw or spoke to her again.

Then in 1992 I received a letter saying that Mom had died, and "by the way, I'm your brother." I asked the guy to send me a picture of himself, which he did, and he looked like me. I was so surprised to see someone who had some of the same physical features that I had. He immediately flew out to California.

His name is Steve Tuers, he lives in Yonkers, New York, where he drives a truck for the United Parcel Service. He's a big, wonderful guy. We've become close. We talk to each other at least once a week. It's been a heartening experience to find that I have a half brother after all these years.

My father also remarried, to a woman named Eloise. They had two daughters. My half sister Lisa has made quite a career out of music. She has a great talent for music, sings, plays several instruments, teaches, and has recorded with Frank Zappa and on her own. She's a sweetheart and I adore her. My other half sister Pamela is a very bright young lady who is in the psychiatric field in Chicago. I'm a good thirty years older than both of them, and am closer to Lisa only because of geography. We both live out West.

Speaking of my dad and Eloise, you may have read about them when they were in the headlines in 1974. She was convicted of attempting to hire two men to kill my father. She served nineteen months of a one-to-five-year sentence. They divorced but he amazingly remarried her later. Sam Popeil died at age sixty-nine of natural causes.

Even though over the years I helped make my father a richer man by selling his products on television, I still never got close to him. He never said he loved me, even when banking his Chop-O-Matic and Veg-O-Matic checks. I never heard the word *love* from any of my relatives. But I do believe he was proud of me. I also believe he loved me in his own way, he just wasn't the sort of person who would say such things out loud. His entertainment was his business. I rarely ever saw him laugh. That kind of tells you something.

My brother Jerry alternately worked for me as a demonstrator and for my father at Popeil Brothers. We tried to take care of him. Jerry died in his mid-forties of a combination of obesity and alcoholism.

CHAPTER 6

My First TV Commercial

Occasionally, after a long day at the fairs, Mel Korey and I would half daydream/half joke about how to make a tough, long job easier. Instead of demonstrating to crowds of ten to a hundred people all day, why not rent a stadium, do one demonstration for sixty to eighty thousand people, and then go home!

Little did we know what was right around the corner. Fantasy turned out to be not all that far from reality thanks to the new medium of television. Suddenly the streets of Chicago were dark in the evening, as everyone was gathered at home in front of these new TV sets, watching Uncle Miltie, Lucy and Ricky, Ralph and Alice, and don't forget the big guys—wrestling.

Texaco, Philip Morris, and DeSoto were reporting big sales for their products thanks to television advertising. And the profits weren't just being generated by the big national companies: small firms were buying local ads and producing them locally for little cost. I wanted to get in on that. What a great way to reach the masses, and I wouldn't have to spend hours slicing and chopping vegetables and fruits (or so I thought at the time).

A friend of mine came by Woolworth's and said, "Ron, I know where you can make a commercial for $550." It was at a station in Tampa, Florida, whose call letters were WFLA; $550 to me was just half a week's pay. What did I have to lose? An airline ticket and $550.

I called the station and they confirmed the price.

So now I needed a product.

I was discussing with a friend, Harry Halperin, what kind of item to sell on TV. We started talking about the various kinds of car wash products that were out there. There was one I liked that used a high pressure nozzle to wash cars; he knew of one that was even better. By inserting different tablets between the hose and the nozzle, it could wash cars, fertilize your lawns, and kill weeds. This was a better mousetrap. Harry tracked the product down for me. He made a commission, and I bought several hundred thousand pieces from the manufacturer, who was based in Chicago.

The Ronco Spray Gun was a great product to begin my TV career with because everyone could use it. You could wash or wax your car and second-story windows too. Then add on the gardening aspects: it killed weeds and bugs and could fertilize your lawn. When you look for a product to take on, you always want to look for something that makes people's lives easier. You also want a product that will keep customers coming back for more. The Spray Gun came with a few tablets, but every time they ran out of a wax or detergent or fertilizer, weed-killer or insecticide-tablet customers would need to visit the store and pick up another pack of five for $2.99. (This is very much like the razor blade business.) That was a great way to keep the profits coming in.

I went to Tampa to film the commercial and stayed with a friend, Marvin Aronovitz. I also used his home—and car—

to film the commercial. I wrote and announced the spot and talked about the high costs of washing and waxing your car, the problems of getting second-story windows clean and how you could stand on the ground and shoot soapy, forced water out of the nozzle to power the dirt off those windows. There never was any thought of hiring professionals to star in the spot. I knew how to announce. That was my background from Woolworth's and fairs.

Then I went to Mel for help in distributing the product. We took some of our money from the fair circuit and established a joint account. In school Mel had helped me in one of my classes. I remembered Mel always helping me whenever I needed it, so when it was time to form a business I wanted to make Mel a 50 percent partner.

Even though I made the commercial in Tampa, we didn't sell it there at first. I was still working at Woolworth's in Chicago and I wanted to stay close to home. We made deals with TV stations and retail stores in Springfield and Rockford, Illinois, and Madison, Wisconsin. It cost money to ship the Spray Guns to Florida. This way we could throw them in the back of our cars and get them to the stores as well as keep close tabs on how things were going.

To help me handle both Woolworth's and the Spray Gun at the same time, my brother pinch-hit for me and I hired other demonstrators as well.

To get us started in retail, Mel and I offered a deal stores couldn't really refuse. We sold our product on a guaranteed-sale basis. That means whatever they couldn't sell, they returned back to us, and we would issue them a refund, because we got paid for the merchandise in full. Don't mistake that for consignment, which is when you ship—not sell—the product to the store. You don't get paid until the product is sold (and have to take their word for how many pieces were sold). If the store burns down, or the merchandise is stolen by a customer, or even an employee of the store, you've lost

THE RONCO SPRAY GUN

"The gun that washes and waxes your car in less than five minutes!"

PROBLEM: *Washing and waxing your car, getting second-story windows clean, and taking care of your garden or lawn.*

While still demonstrating products at Woolworth's in Chicago, I began my first entry into the TV marketing business. It all began because I wanted to take advantage of the new medium of television. A friend told me about a TV station in Tampa, Florida, where you could make commercials for $550. Another pal told me about a new garden accessory that could wash your car and fertilize your lawn and that sounded to me like a perfect TV product.

•

We went to the Chicago-based manufacturer, and I bought a small quantity, which eventually grew to several hundred thousand pieces. I named it the Ronco Spray Gun and began advertising them on TV, in Springfield and Rockford, Illinois, and Madison, Wisconsin.

•

We eventually went national and sold nearly 1 million Spray Guns in four years.

out because the merchandise really never changed ownership.

Consignment stinks, and guaranteed sale isn't much better because store owners are hesitant to trust you to send
them back the money for returned merchandise like you're
supposed to. But at least it's a way to get in the door.

When we went to a store and offered to sell our products
on a guaranteed-sale basis, the store couldn't lose anything.
At least that's the impression we tried to convey to them. We
also convinced them that while we were advertising our
product on TV, we would also tell viewers to buy our product at their store. And while the customer would be buying
our product, they would also buy other products while in
their store. Not a bad sales presentation.

I've gotten credit for being the innovator of marketing
products on television, but it's not all totally deserved. Yes, I
was one of the first to advertise products on television, but I
assure you, anybody who put a decent product on TV with
a good commercial (it didn't have to be great) would have
made a lot of money on TV back when I started. TV was so
new, and so few local products (silver cleaners, hair and
kitchen items mostly) were being advertised. I was just lucky
to be in the right place at the right time. In those days you
could advertise empty boxes on television and sell them. It
was hard not to be successful.

The Spray Gun ad worked in Springfield and it worked
in Madison. Now I wanted Mel to go out on the road and
sign up other stores, using the guaranteed-sale TV concept
that we had set up. And it was a great concept. The store got
free advertising and added traffic. While with our "guaranteed sale" the stores made less of a markup—25 percent
rather than the normal 40 percent on our products—they
could return what they didn't sell. Theoretically, they had no
risk.

While I made the TV commercials and demonstrated the

product at stores, Mel went from city to city, store to store, setting up new retail accounts, and buying TV advertising time from the stations using my TV commercial.

Eventually we had the Spray Gun in a hundred cities, advertised on local TV stations because that's where the bargain TV time was. Mel was great at striking up solid relationships with the stations and stores. I don't look at myself as someone who wins popularity contests. I'm the kind of guy people either like or hate, no in-between. But everybody loves Mel. And he was in the right place at the right time. By making him a 50 percent owner of Ronco, we both went on to receive $2.5 million each when the company went public in 1969. And Mel earned every dollar of it. He went out and got us into retail and onto many TV stations while I developed new products and commercials. It was a great partnership.

Doing my first TV commercial was quite a wake-up call. The same sales pitch that I was doing for one person could be accomplished with the same effort on TV. And here I could talk to hundreds of thousands of people with no strain on my voice and I wouldn't be exhausted at the end of the day. Not to mention that my sales would be many thousand times more than the single pitch, with the same amount of effort.

CHAPTER 7

Chop-O-Matic

Once the money was pouring in for the Ronco Spray Gun, we naturally wanted a sequel. We were already buying TV ad time for one product and achieving great results; why not buy TV time for another product too?

The second product came from my dad—a revolutionary kitchen device called the Chop-O-Matic. He saw the success I was having with the Spray Gun, came to me, and said "Ron, I want you to sell the Chop-O-Matic. This is your cost, this is what you should be selling it for. Sound good?" Sure, Dad.

The Chop-O-Matic was a food chopper with rotating blades ("Chops in seven seconds or less.") It was revolutionary for doing so many different things and was a great time-saver for the family meal-maker.

Before I went on TV with the Chop-O-Matic, I spent several weeks selling the product at Woolworth's. After several days of demonstrating the product, I learned what features consumers were particularly interested in and what kind of questions they would ask.

I never considered writing a script for the Chop-O-Matic commercial. Why bother? If I've been chopping away for ten hours a day, giving the same pitch over and over again, refining it a little bit each time, who needs a script? I could operate the machine blindfolded. So for the first TV spot (a five-minute commercial, or mini-infomercial) I just did the same demonstration I'd been doing at Woolworth's, compressing everything for TV that I'd learned from my sales pitch.

My arrangement with my father was strictly financial. He sold me Chop-O-Matics at the same wholesale price he would sell to any other middleman. I sold them at Woolworth's as a pitchman, but wondered what would happen one day if I wasn't available to pitch. How would I make money? I always knew I could get behind a counter, whether at Woolworth's or at the state fair, come rain or shine, earn a living, and live the lifestyle of a well-off individual. But God help me if something happened and I couldn't get behind the counter. Then what?

So Mel and I decided to try something novel: We would advertise the Chop-O-Matic on TV, but make it available to TV viewers only via mail order. Like today, when I direct consumers to call 1-800-43-RONCO, then I had consumers send a check or money order to the TV station or a post office box. And then we would ship the product out to them. I guess you could call this the first infomercial, because I made deals with local stations to run longer-than-usual ads—usually two minutes—and we had viewers call a phone number to order.

Chop-O-Matic was the biggest success my father had ever seen in his life. Once we put the product on TV, we were selling thousands of units. Flush with newfound dollars, my father started dreaming up Chop-O-Matic sequels. First

THE CHOP-O-MATIC

"Ladies and Gentlemen, I'm going to show you the greatest kitchen appliance ever made!"

PROBLEM: *Teary eyes.*

With those words I launched, on television, the product that really got my father and me off and running in the late 1950s. The Chop-O-Matic was a simple chopping device that cut up vegetables, potatoes, and meats.

●

I sold the product at fairs and Woolworth's, but after I got such great response to the Ronco Spray Gun on television, my father asked me, on behalf of one of his other customers, to also sell the Chop-O-Matic on television, via mail order. The ad was primitive by today's standards—a black-and-white image of me at a kitchen counter with the Chop-O-Matic. There were no audiences, or multicameras, or the beautiful sets like we have today. I simply demonstrated all the different things the product could do.

●

At the fairs, besides not being able to talk at the end of the day, because my throat and lungs would be so tired from twelve hours of nonstop talking, the palm of my hand would also be extremely sore from the continuous pounding of the food chopper.

●

"Many of you remember these old relics like that old chopping bowl and that old knuckle grater. There's no place in your kitchen for these horse-and-buggy utensils any longer. The Chop-O-Matic is a brand new, revolutionary invention. Instead of wasting time cutting a celery with a knife as you usually would, place the celery under the chopper. It's just like bouncing a ball."

●

(I kept the Grandma bit going. . . .)

●

"Everyone likes cole slaw—everyone, that is, except Mother. The reason she doesn't like it is because she's the one who has to make it on that old grater, and, oh, the scrapes on her poor knuckles. Well, here's where your Chop-O-Matic comes to the rescue. Place that cabbage under the container and start tapping. And just look at how fine this cole slaw is made."

●

(You'll notice how I waited until the end to ask for the money.)

•

"I know you're all wondering what this machine sells for. Well, Chop-O-Matic will be nationally advertised for $5.98, and it's well worth it. But during this special TV presentation, if you order right now, the price is not $5.98, but $3.98. That's right, just $3.98! And, as a special bonus, you will receive with your Chop-O-Matic at no additional charge, a valuable recipe book—'50 Secret Recipes by World Famous Chefs.' "

•

In all candor, I really don't remember where all those world famous chefs came from.

came the Dial-O-Matic, another slicer. But unlike the Slice-A-Way, another of my father's earlier products, the Dial-O-Matic had a safety guard to prevent you from cutting yourself. On the Dial-O-Matic, you could vary the thickness of the slice by turning a dial.

Then came my father's greatest invention, one whose name I've been associated with ever since. The Veg-O-Matic, the product that "slices and dices and juliennes to perfection."

For only $9.99 consumers got a small product that was unusually versatile. It did slice, did dice, and did wedge just about anything. And TV viewers went crazy when they saw the ad that I did for the product. People lined up in housewares departments, fighting over who got to buy the last one in stock. Over 11 million Veg-O-Matics were sold, the all-time best for my dad and uncle.

Some thirteen years after its introduction, the Veg-O-Matic was still so fondly remembered that Dan Aykroyd did a takeoff on the product on *Saturday Night Live,* with the "Bass-O-Matic '76," the blender that chopped, sliced, and diced—fish. I loved it.

Veg-O-Matic was Ronco's second retail product. We bought them from my father and then Mel and I turned around and sold them to stores like Woolworth's, Walgreen's, and Eckerd's Drugs.

The way the deals worked back then was that my ad would direct consumers to buy it specifically at one of the above stores. So I was spending money strictly to get customers to X or Y store. Other stores might also carry the Veg-O-Matic, but they were supplied by others.

Ronco became bigger and hotter and we expanded beyond my father's kitchen gadgets. We embarked on other products that weren't manufactured by him, most notably stockings (London Aire Hosiery). Because of our constant TV exposure everybody and their brother started proposing products to us that they felt could be instant TV hits.

My cousin Nat Morris, for instance, used to send us crazy concoctions every month or so, which, for some reason, he would always name after a cigarette. There was the Winston Hemmer and Stitcher (a portable sewing machine), the Chesterfield Knife Set, and the L & M Grater and Sifter. I never wanted to take one on, but one of Nat's proposals did have me in stitches: the Newport combination denture washer and milkshake maker. His reasoning? People who wear dentures are self-conscious, but if you add the milkshake feature, the clerk at the checkout counter won't know what you're buying it for. This whole concept was ridiculous to me and made no sense.

We still continued to work the fairs, although they became less and less important for us as our TV business became stronger. Mel's problem was that he always needed to be by

💡 THE DIAL-O-MATIC

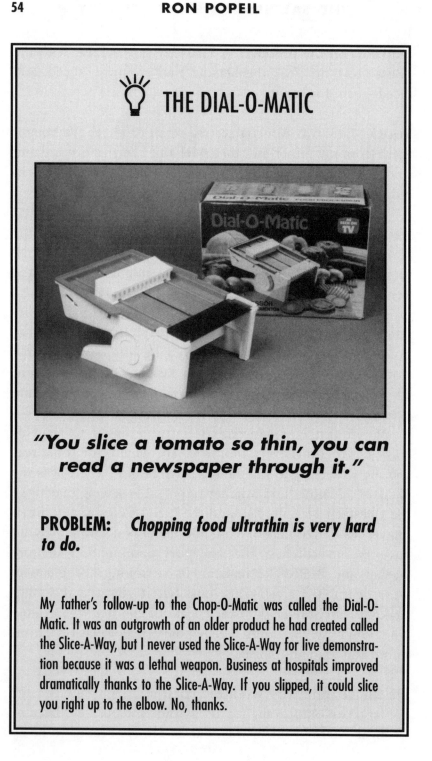

"You slice a tomato so thin, you can read a newspaper through it."

PROBLEM: *Chopping food ultrathin is very hard to do.*

My father's follow-up to the Chop-O-Matic was called the Dial-O-Matic. It was an outgrowth of an older product he had created called the Slice-A-Way, but I never used the Slice-A-Way for live demonstration because it was a lethal weapon. Business at hospitals improved dramatically thanks to the Slice-A-Way. If you slipped, it could slice you right up to the elbow. No, thanks.

•

Next was a much better product, the Dial-O-Matic food slicer. We didn't take it on television right away, because we were still making lots of money with the Chop-O-Matics, but I did sell the product at Woolworth's and on the fair circuit. The Dial-O-Matic had a dial on it, and you could dial and regulate the slicing from thin to medium to thick. It also had the ability to shoestring your vegetables as well as waffle them. I used to hold up two waffle potatoes under my ears and say, "If you don't want to eat them, they certainly make beautiful earrings."

•

I also used to say, "When tomatoes get expensive in the wintertime, the Ronco Dial-O-Matic food slicer can cut tomotoes so thin, you can make one tomato last you all winter long. You can slice a tomato so thin with the Dial-O-Matic that the tomato only has one side!"

•

Most of the old Ronco choppers and slicers aren't around today, but we still make the Dial-O-Matic. In fact we give it away with the Ronco Electric Food Dehydrator. It's an extra bonus, something extra to give customers that is, in fact, associated with the product they're buying. One of the prerequisites in drying foods is to slice your food very thin. So there's a perfect tie-in.

•

"Crinkle cuts, lattice cuts, dice cuts, thin cuts, julienne cuts, waffle cuts, cole slaw cuts, and strip cuts . . . all for just $7.77!"

a phone in case one of our accounts called with a question or wanted to order. I solved that problem by installing a phone at his fair booth, on the same counter where he was demonstrating.

Here was Mel with fifty to a hundred people in front of

him. Just as he was about to ask for the first ten or twelve people in his audience to purchase his product, the phone would ring. He had to pick it up, and basically lost all the people who were ready to buy.

This just didn't work.

My father prided himself on inventing consumer products. He utilized me because of my selling ability. So now that we were making lots of money for him, did our relationship change? Not really. Did he ever say thanks for moving all those Chop-O-Matics, Veg-O-Matics, and Dial-O-Matics for him? Never.

Before my father passed away, though, he was living in Miami, and I needed some money to do a transaction on something and my funds were tied up at the time. "Dad," I said, "I need half a million dollars." He looked at his wife, Eloise, and said, "Give him what he needs." That he would think enough of me to lend me half a million dollars said a lot. I viewed this as his small way of saying he respected and trusted me.

CHAPTER 8

High Finances

I learned my trade on the streets but I've always regretted not having a formal education. How much more successful could I have been had I finished college?

Look at what education did for my friend Steve Wynn, Chairman of Mirage Resorts in Las Vegas. He's driven like I'm driven and could probably come into my business and fare even better than I have because of his educational background. It's hard not to admire the business skills and scholastic knowledge he obtained at Wharton Business School. And when you look at the bottom line and how much money he's made versus how much money I've made, well . . . I've got a *long, long* way to go to catch up with him.

Had I continued with higher education, I might have gotten into the worlds of IPOs, stocks, and bonds earlier than I did. Either way, going public was a great move for Ronco, Ron Popeil, and Mel Korey. All thanks to a friend, Bill Gruenberg, who made a very interesting suggestion to me one day.

It was 1968, in Aspen, and Bill—who made his living by playing the stock market—and I were lounging in a Jacuzzi. We were sitting outside, surrounded by snow, and chatting about the old days when we were in school together.

Bill asked how my business was going. Ronco was coming off its fourth great year in a row, growing from $200,000 in sales to $8.8 million. Bill was quite impressed.

"Ron, have you ever considered taking your company public?" he asked me.

"What's that?" I said. I was thirty-four years old at the time, and I really didn't know what going public meant.

So Bill went on to explain it to me. "Look, Ron, we can take this company of yours and sell a small portion of it to the public. I have contacts at some investment banking firms. Let me investigate it for you."

Bill, who had many connections in the investment banking area, had convinced Shearson Hammill to meet with us to be our potential underwriter for a public offering. They targeted the summer of 1969 for the offering and recommended that we change the name of our company. Ronco, they said, didn't really say anything about who we were. (Sure it did: Ron's Company.) They wanted a name that was descriptive of what we did. So we became Ronco Teleproducts.

When the offering went through in August, Mel and I became multimillionaires overnight. The public paid $5.5 million for 22 percent of Ronco Teleproducts, which Mel and I split. Going public and getting so much money for a small slice of your company is a pretty nice thing to have happen to you, especially for a guy who grew up on chicken feet and bean soup.

When Mel and I were nineteen years old, we made a pact with each other, as kids tend to do. If we ever make any big money, we're going to have some really big wagers. We had just both received checks for $2.5 million from Shearson

Hammill. And reminding Mel of the bets we had planned earlier in our lives, I said to Mel, "It's time for our first big bet." And he said, "How much is it going to be?" And I responded, "$40,000." He said to me, "If you win, Ron, what do you want for your $40,000?" I replied, "I've always wanted a sailboat. I used to watch them in Chicago. I was always fascinated by sailboats. I didn't know how to sail, but that's what I want." And what did Mel want if he won? And I have to admit, to this day, that his answer was a better answer. He said, "I'll take the cash."

After the offering I walked into his office and said, "Okay, Mel. Odds or evens, one shot." I put my right hand in the air, ready to throw probably one finger out. He looked at me and looked at my arm in its cocked position and said, "No, Ron. Let's flip a coin." But I was prepared. I pulled a two-headed coin out of my pocket, flipped it in the air, and said, "Call it, Mel." His call was tails. And I was the recipient of a $40,000 sailboat, which really cost me an additional $15,000 because of the boat I wanted. As I left the office, I threw him the coin. He caught it and looked at it. He looked at both sides, and he smiled. He didn't complain. From my point of view, he was the one who had requested the flip of the coin and he was the one who had called it. I knew Mel. It was obvious. I knew the way Mel would react. I named the boat *Korey's Loss.*

In 1970 we had another, smaller offering, this time on the American Stock Exchange, worth $750,000. And it was time for another big bet. This bet was for a Rolls-Royce. This time, I lost the bet. I asked Mel what kind of Rolls-Royce he wanted. I know if I had won, it would have been a new one, but Mel said, "I want a Silver Cloud." Now, there were no new Silver Clouds. So we had to find Mel a used Silver Cloud. Which I did. And it cost me about $15,000. The irony of it is that Mel loved the way it looked and didn't complain that it was used. But Mel being Mel, he refused to

THE VEG-O-MATIC

"Slices and dices and juliennes to perfection."

PROBLEM: *The time and effort it can take to slice, dice, and wedge with an ordinary knife.*

For most of my career people have assumed that I went on television and said, "The Veg-O-Matic. It slices! It dices!" But that's not so.

•

Let me clear this up right now. Like Cary Grant, who never said, "Judy, Judy, Judy," or Humphrey Bogart in *Casablanca*, who never told the piano player to "Play it again, Sam," I never said, "It slices! It dices!" for the Veg-O-Matic. I swear!

●

The Veg-O-Matic, probably my father's greatest invention ever, was a product that sliced, diced, and wedged. The only lines I used on TV about slicing and dicing had to do with onions. "When slicing or dicing onions, the only tears you'll shed will be tears of joy."

●

I'm using that same phrase today on TV with the Dial-O-Matic demonstration!

●

For those who don't believe that I never said, "It slices! It dices!" in the commercial, here's the transcript:

●

"This is Veg-O-Matic, the world famous food appliance. Slice a whole potato into uniform slices with one motion. Hamburger lovers, feed whole onions into the Veg-O-Matic and make these tempting thin slices. Simply turn the ring and change from thin to thick slices. Isn't that amazing? Like magic, you can change from slicing to dicing. No one likes dicing onions. The Veg-O-Matic makes mounds of them fast. The only tears you'll shed will be tears of joy. You can make hundreds of French fries in one minute. Isn't that sensational? Here's your chance to own one for only $9.99. At no extra cost we'll throw in this extra booklet of recipes from world famous chefs."

●

The Veg-O-Matic was my third TV product, after the Ronco Spray Gun and Chop-O-Matic. The year was 1963, and the product wasn't sold via mail order, but instead at retail. Business was incredible. People would be lined up in the store to buy the product at Christmastime and get into fights over who could buy the last remaining unit.

●

The Veg-O-Matic was so clever. It had several different blades locked in an aluminum ring that could be adjusted instantly to vary the thickness of the slice. You could put a whole potato in for a French-fry cut. With a turn of the ring you could be making julienne potatoes. A separate ring was used for lemon wedges.

•

The results from the TV ads were simply spectacular. The Veg-O-Matic was my dad's most successful product ever. We sold 11 million units, which brought in a lot of potatoes for him and myself. We don't sell it today because there are too many motorized products out there that can do the same thing a lot faster and much easier. But in its time it was really something.

•

"Save money by ordering Veg-O-Matic now, while it's still available, at just $7.77."

have a chauffeur. And the seat could not be positioned to deal with Mel's tall body. So when he drove it, his stomach appeared to be touching the wheel. He was obviously cramped every time he rode in his winning Rolls-Royce. After a short time Mel traded this Rolls in on a new one, for which he footed the bill. My kinda guy!

As Ronco grew, we brought in more and more executives to help run the firm, and Mel and I concentrated on our strengths. I dwelled on product development and making TV commercials. Mel ran Castle Advertising, our in-house ad agency, which was set up to buy TV advertising time for us. (By going in-house, we didn't have to pay a 15 percent commission to outside agencies.)

We were constantly bringing out new products, because the stores demanded that from us. They always wanted something new. A product had a shelf life as long as the store wanted to carry it. Why did the Veg-O-Matic disappear from sight? Not because consumers had stopped buying it. The stores got tired of looking at it and wanted to make room for the next hit, the next item that would draw customers in.

People are always developing new stuff to compete for shelf space. I should know. That's what I do every day. And the retail store buyer is king. If you don't comply with his or her wishes, you're out in the cold. You could have the greatest product in the world, but if you can't get into the marketplace, you're dead. It's like giving someone $1 million on a desert island. If he can't spend it, what good is the money?

It's a different situation with infomercials. You can stay on the air as long as you're willing to keep paying the costs of media.

My father's relationship with his partner and brother Ray was somewhat similar to mine with Mel. Sam created the products and Ray sold them. I created the products and developed the advertising and Mel bought the TV time and sold to the stores.

My uncle Ray came from the same school as my grandfather, the school of hard knocks. Ray was as friendly to me as my grandfather—which is to say not very. But he did appreciate the fact that I made lots of money for him at Popeil Brothers. Once I started branching out, and taking on products that weren't made by them, he felt quite different about me. He never said anything to me about how upset he was, he simply figured he'd get even by refusing to speak to me. In fact the man didn't talk to me for twenty-five years. My dad was a wealthy man and never got on my case for developing my own product.

In fact, after doing so well with our public offerings, I showed my father and uncle how they could go public, too, and they pocketed millions, just like I did. The only negative is that on Wall Street, and in Chicago, my father became known as Ron Popeil's dad. Which really wasn't fair. He was a great innovator and achieved a lot in his life. He invented a great many amazing consumer products. I marketed them and without those inventions I would have had to develop or find their replacements.

Besides the instant millions we achieved from going public, I also learned a great deal about Americans and their investing habits. I discovered that people would pay an inordinate amount of money for the future. Investing in stocks is a form of gambling. You're not buying a product and taking it home and using it. People buy the stock and hope the profits will increase and their gamble will pay off. This is just another form of gambling.

CHAPTER 9

Bankruptcy

By 1984 Ronco had sold records, choppers, slicers, dicers, hosiery, microphones, button machines, pottery and candle kits, salad spinners, and much more, but the end was about to come for the company. After twenty years in business we were forced into bankruptcy.

Did sales go down the drain? No. Did we take our eye off the ball? Probably. Was it a truly unfortunate set of circumstances? Most definitely. Here is one instance where I certainly wasn't in the right place at the right time.

I always did business with the First National Bank of Chicago. They treated me right. I never had to sign for anything personally. The bank went out of its way to extend loans for Ronco when we needed capital to expand.

Our borrowing kept creeping up to the point where in the early 1980s it was up to $15 million. Our arrangement with the bank was like a revolving line of credit. We would pay the interest and roll over what we had borrowed. We kept just turning it over and over.

In the early 1980s another Chicago bank had a very serious financial problem. The federal government had to bail them out. Their woes affected First National. When one giant bank experiences trouble, another bank starts to say, "Well, wait a second. We better reexamine what we're doing. Are we doing business in the same fashion as this other bank? Let's take a good look at our loans."

The individuals who had been loaning us money over the years were all replaced by new people. And the new loan officers took a dim view of Ronco products. "We're loaning you $15 million for these little gadgets?" To them they were gadgets, but to me they represented tens of millions of dollars in sales and profits.

In November we got the bad news. Despite the fact that we always paid off our loans or rolled them over with the bank taking its interest, First National Bank called and said our loan would have to be settled by January. No more revolving line of credit.

This was a major problem. Our products were sold to stores on a guaranteed sale basis and retailers didn't pay us for the Christmas products until around April. How in the world would we ever be able to pay off the loan in January? I didn't know. I thought someone would rescue us somehow. But that didn't happen.

Here's what we did: The loan was guaranteed, not by me personally, but by the inventory of the company and the accounts receivable. So in January they asked for their money and I said we didn't have it. They said, "Okay, then, we're going to take your receivables and we now own your inventory."

So the bank and lawyers took over the account receivables, and as some of the invoices from Christmas were paid, they got the money. Meanwhile, a major supplier for our company called me looking for his money (I owed him about $500,000). I couldn't pay him, because the bank was getting all the money. He forced me into Chapter 11 bankruptcy.

Ronco was being forced out of business, primarily because of problems at a lending institution that I had never done business with, Continental Bank of Chicago.

First National was taking most of the money, I couldn't buy TV time that I wanted to buy, suppliers wouldn't supply me with goods because of our lack of funds. It was a mess. In a couple of years we were in Chapter 7 bankruptcy and out of business. The bank got all the Ronco inventory, including a warehouse full of goods that had come back from guaranteed sale.

Fortunately I wasn't hurt too badly. When the bank took over Ronco, they still paid me $1,000 a week. It was a lot less than I had been making, and other perks were taken away. But did I lose money personally? No. If I had tied myself up by giving personal guarantees, they could have come after my personal assets and wiped me out. Luckily I never did.

To recoup the money still owed to them, the bank decided to auction off all the inventory they had legal possession of. I saw an opportunity here to make something positive out of a bad situation. I knew what to do with the merchandise, nobody else did. So I made the bank a verbal offer.

"I don't know what you're going to get for this public auction, but I'm not going to be there because everybody would watch my bidding, and I'm not going to have that happen. Tell you what I'd like to do. I'll buy all the inventory for $2 million in cash. Personally."

The bank said they'd get back to me.

They held the auction and tentatively sold off all the individual products—which included the CleanAire Machine and the Ronco Electric Food Dehydrator.

(A collective bid would supersede the individual bids.)

At the end of the day they were up to $1.2 million on the individual bids. The bank representative called and said, "Ron, you said you would give $2 million as a collective bid for all the merchandise." I could have said, "Well, you have offers for $1.2 million. I'll give you $1.4 million." But I didn't. I stuck to my word. And now I owned the inventory of Ronco again. The tooling alone for the products was worth millions. I got the tooling back too. It was a great deal.

Meanwhile, Mel Korey retired from the business. When the bank took over, they decided they didn't need him anymore. So he moved to Scottsdale, Arizona, and opened up an advertising agency.

I took in a former Ronco salesperson, Malcolm Sherman, as a partner. We got my $2 million back quickly by liquidating a part of the inventory, and there were still millions of dollars of product left.

Still, I felt really bad that it all had to end this way. Some of the shareholders really got hurt. I was hurt the most because I had the largest block of stock. I had made a lot of money via the stock market, but my name got hurt by being associated with a bankruptcy.

I took a lemon and turned it into lemonade. I took the Food Dehydrator and CleanAire Machine and went out there and made money off them.

As it turned out, Malcolm and I didn't see eye to eye on the business so we split three years later. I took the dehydrator and the company with its assets; he got the CleanAire Machine, and I was now a solo act. Like the phoenix who rises from the ashes, I returned with my little Food Dehydrator a few years later and generated sales of over $100 million via infomercials.

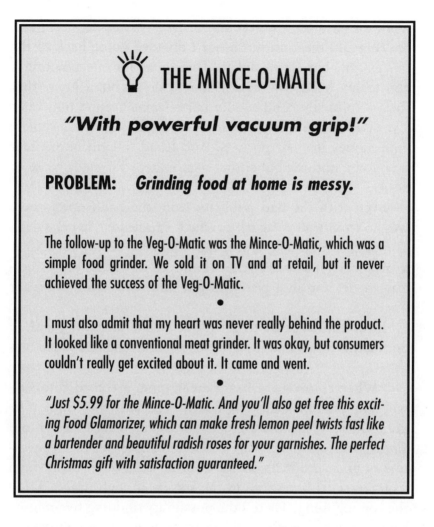

THE MINCE-O-MATIC

"With powerful vacuum grip!"

PROBLEM: *Grinding food at home is messy.*

The follow-up to the Veg-O-Matic was the Mince-O-Matic, which was a simple food grinder. We sold it on TV and at retail, but it never achieved the success of the Veg-O-Matic.

•

I must also admit that my heart was never really behind the product. It looked like a conventional meat grinder. It was okay, but consumers couldn't really get excited about it. It came and went.

•

"Just $5.99 for the Mince-O-Matic. And you'll also get free this exciting Food Glamorizer, which can make fresh lemon peel twists fast like a bartender and beautiful radish roses for your garnishes. The perfect Christmas gift with satisfaction guaranteed."

But first, I had to return to my roots. I had so much inventory. How to get rid of it? By going back to the fair circuit, the perfect place to dispose of inventory. Still it was depressing. I had gone from being the CEO of a publicly traded firm to working in hundred-degree temperature in buildings that weren't even air conditioned, and I was there for twelve or thirteen hours a day. Every day.

Who wants to get up at five A.M. at this stage of life, set up and prepare foods so they look good on the counter, work all day, get a quick bite at Denny's, go to sleep, and return again the next morning? I dreaded going back to the fair circuit, but I still did it. There was no one pointing a gun to my head who said I had to do it, but I knew that shows—plus state and county fairs—came around only once a year, and with them, hundreds of thousands of consumers with money in their pockets. And I had this inventory that was doing nothing but sitting in storage, so it made sense to do it.

Even with the bad publicity from the bankruptcy there was no trouble moving the product. People love to get a deal. You offer a food dehydrator that had been selling for $50 at a fair for $7, it's Underwriters Laboratories approved, American made, and in a beautiful gift box, who wouldn't want it?

It took three years to get rid of all the inventory, and all during this time I had my eyes set on returning in a much bigger way.

"When someone writes a great song, a record company will sign him to a long-term contract because they think if he did it once, he'll write a great song again. That's me," I told *Chicago* magazine in 1987. "I'll introduce another generation of great products one of these days. It won't be through [commercials] like those in the sixties, though. Cable TV is the coming thing. There's the possibility of doing five-minute spots on cable; not just thirty seconds but five minutes. In five minutes I can sell anything. Five minutes for me is a chance to mine gold."

Little did I fathom what was ahead of me.

And what great life lessons did I learn from this whole nasty experience? That outside forces over which we have no control whatsoever can control our destiny. And I can tell you that the smartest move I ever made in my life was not personally guaranteeing anything myself. Personal guarantees can wipe you out. If you come from a background of having nothing and then making all this money, you want to make sure no one can take it away from you. Since I didn't put myself at risk the bank couldn't go after my personal assets.

CHAPTER **10**

Las Vegas

From 1987 to 1990 I was in semiretirement. I worked on developing new products, sold products to other companies, and was asked to join the board of directors of the publicly traded Golden Nugget, which is now called the Mirage Resorts in Las Vegas.

My Las Vegas connection began courtesy of Hallmark's Mother's Day imagery. Mel Korey and I had been going to Las Vegas every Mother's Day for years. We went because of Mel's superstition. If we didn't go—we might have bad luck. Also we always encouraged people to buy our gifts as Mother's Day presents. It was a painful piece of irony, since my mother had dumped me, and his mom had been dead for many years. We thought of the holiday—people taking their moms out, buying them gifts, restaurants crowded with families—and we weren't a part of it. On top of that, when we started going to Vegas we were both either divorced or going through a breakup, so the lack of family was magnified.

THE FEATHER TOUCH KNIFE

"So sharp it could shave the eyebrows off a New Jersey mosquito!"

PROBLEM: *Dull knives.*

Today, everyone knows the Ginsu Knife, the product that can also chop wood and cut a nail—or frozen food—in half. In fact, many people think I sold the Ginsu on TV. Well, the answer to that is yes and no. Back in the 1960s I marketed a product called the Feather Touch Knife, and we bought it from the same company that currently makes the Ginsu, the Kwikcut Company of Columbus, Ohio.

•

We sold our knives ("so sharp you could cut a cow in half, and that's no bull") for $2.98 at fairs and retail, and it, like the Ginsu, could also cut nails, leather, wood, and still slice a ripe red tomato paper thin. The only thing that's changed in the years between the Feather Touch Knife and the Ginsu is the price—it now sells for around $30, and they also throw in six steak knives.

•

"Get one today, and receive this fabulous fork-tipped carver also. Now you can carve roast beef just like a professional. Remember, you get not one, but two knives for $2.98."

Las Vegas was a good place to get away from all of that and have a great time.

I had met the Mirage's CEO, Stephen Wynn, through an old Chicago friend, Michael Pascal, whose sister Elaine was married to Steve. I would occasionally run into them while in Vegas.

During one of my visits to town, solo this time, Steve approached me about joining his board. He was familiar with my background in successful marketing as well as running a public company. He wanted me to be an "outside director," someone who could also represent the shareholders.

I didn't know what exactly to expect. Of course, Ronco had its own board of directors (I was chairman of that board), but I wasn't an expert about the gaming business. However, business is basically business. You're dealing with profits and people; marketing and sales.

I thought about it and wanted to do it because it was a different kind of business. It was a challenge and also a compliment. In my opinion, and in many others', the Mirage is the premier gaming operation in the world. It's certainly the most beautiful and luxurious. That's the way Steve Wynn has always done things. First class. Even in downtown Las Vegas, which had traditionally been the honky-tonk part of town, Steve shocked locals when he transformed the Golden Nugget from an old-fashioned "gambling hall" to a classy resort for the affluent. It was the opposite of any of his garish neighbors, with understated white decor, imported white trees, and no neon sign.

Being a director at the Mirage has been one of the greatest experiences of my life, because it connected me to Stephen Wynn. Some of the other directors are George Mason, a partner in Bear Stearns; Boone Watson, a Maryland real estate entrepreneur; Skip Bronson, who works for the Mirage in the area of new jurisdictions, and has a background in shopping centers; and Mel Wolzinger, the Mirage's second-largest shareholder and an old friend of Steve's.

I made my success selling kitchen products on TV. The contacts I had were other pitchmen, carnies, and the like. I had never come into contact with these kinds of movers and shakers before.

Many of you probably don't remember the days before the Mirage and Treasure Island went up. Back then it was just a large collection of sand in the desert, in between Caesars Palace and the Fashion Show Mall. At that time the land was owned by the Summa Corporation, Howard Hughes's company that used to own many big Vegas hotels, including the Desert Inn, where Hughes himself lived for four years, the Sands, the Landmark, and the Frontier. In the 1980s Summa got out of the gaming business, selling off each property, piece by piece, and the land became available. I was instrumental in helping Steve buy the property.

Steve had made an offer of $60 million for the land, but Summa rejected it. "Does anybody have any other ideas?" Steve asked.

Summa's problem with our bid was that we put contingencies into the deal. There was a gas station and a gift shop on the land, and we wanted Summa to take care of them before we took ownership. I suggested a counterproposal. How about we offer $50 million, with no contingencies? We'll take on the responsibility of dealing with those property owners ourselves. And Summa accepted.

So now, every time I pass the Mirage, I smile, knowing that I had something to do with the Mirage sitting where it is today. And I can't tell you how exciting it is to work with Steve and watch him conduct his business. I may be an expert at marketing, but Steve is a genius at running a business. I believe he's making history in Las Vegas.

Whatever Steve touches turns to gold. He has a phenomenal mind and expertise in so many areas. It's almost like he can see the future. He's like me: An idea doesn't remain an idea for long. He makes it happen.

I design products for TV; he designs casinos, structures, restaurants, packaging, music, and he's even an announcer. If you go to the Mirage, you'll hear his voice talking about the property as you enter; he also does the in-house video in all the rooms that talk about the features of the Mirage.

Becoming so involved with the Mirage, I decided to move to Las Vegas. I'm on various Mirage committees and I take the director's post very seriously, so I need to be around. It's enjoyable and I am learning from some very smart people. I have a Ronco office in Las Vegas as well, but my work in town is split between my business and the Mirage. The only negative part about residing in Las Vegas is that it can get awfully hot there during the summer. But in the winter the weather is delightful and it doesn't hurt to be associated with the top casino resort hotel in the world.

The Comeback

It was my old friend Mike Srednick who brought me out of semiretirement. I've known Mike since the 1960s. He was a customer of my father's and, like me, he bought product from Popeil Brothers, advertised it on TV, and sold the items to retail outlets.

But it wasn't until I moved west that I really got to know Mike. Today he is one of my closest friends in the world. I wish my marriages had been as good as my relationship with Mike.

In California my life was turned around again when Mike suggested I go back to TV marketing with home shopping and infomercials. He had some connections with Fingerhut, one of America's largest mail-order houses, and was able to set up a meeting for us there.

Fingerhut is based in Minneapolis, and they do nearly $2 billion a year in business, mostly on the strength of their catalogs. At that time they were looking for a way to expand their small TV home-shopping business, which was in its infancy. QVC and Home Shopping Network were new and hot, and infomercials had just begun.

Most of the early infomercials back then were how to get rich by buying real estate with no money down, how to work out of your home, things like that. Not my favorite kind of television. I've never known anyone who ever purchased a get-rich program off TV and made the kind of money that was promised.

Anyway, Mike and I met with several Fingerhut executives. At the time Fingerhut owned a subsidiary company called USA Direct, which ran a small shopping show on satellite. The programming was available to people in rural areas who couldn't get cable and watched TV via their satellite dish. USA Direct's shopping show was similar to what you see today on QVC or the Home Shopping Network, except that it was on a much smaller scale. It came on at three P.M. and was off by ten P.M.

Fingerhut liked what I was selling and the way I sold it. They agreed to buy 20,000 Food Dehydrators with a six-month TV home-shopping exclusive for the product, if I would agree to go on their show to sell them. This deal to me was a slam dunk. Besides the TV exposure, they also agreed to put my product in their catalogs. I couldn't lose.

At the time, most orders on their home-shopping show were duds: threes and fours. When I went on with the Food Dehydrator, I sold 232 units on the first day! To them these were big-time numbers and they could easily predict the future.

I didn't know at the time that losses at the satellite operation were hurting the profits at Fingerhut, whose board of directors decided to get rid of USA Direct. So our deal wasn't going to go anywhere at the end of six months.

This was 1991.

We were going to work with Fingerhut to do an infomercial for the Food Dehydrator, but when they dumped

USA Direct, they decided not to pursue it. So I went ahead and did it on my own. I rented a studio, got a hostess and all the things necessary (cameraman, sound, et cetera), booked an audience, and did twenty-eight minutes and thirty seconds for the Ronco Electric Food Dehydrator.

The total production cost was $33,000. For everything— talent, audience, production, and editing. This was my reentry to the TV sales business after so many years.

I had appeared on camera in my earliest ads, but later had preferred to let the product be the star. I still did the voice-overs. Why pay for an announcer or a celebrity? I stepped behind the scenes because I wanted viewers to focus on the product, not on the individual selling it. Because of that, most people knew the name Ronco better than Ron Popeil.

For the Food Dehydrator infomercial I changed my policy about appearing on camera, because now it was a whole new ball game. The infomercial was an arena of pitchmen: Anthony Robbins, Mike Levey, Wally Nash, the Juiceman. It was a perfect avenue for an inventor to be on camera and talk about his product. And with twenty-eight minutes and thirty seconds to fill (not thirty minutes as most people think), it's impossible just to continue showing close-ups of your product. The infomercial is an entertainment type of commercial. You can interact with the audience, just like you do at the state fair; you can have fun showing all the things the product can do. I had finally found the perfect medium.

Our infomercial wasn't scripted, but we did have a very loose outline. The name of the show was *Incredible Inventions,* and we opened with a parade of past hits (The Veg-O-Matic, Buttoneer, Pocket Fisherman, Bottle and Jar Cutter, Mr. Dentist, and Mr. Microphone, to name a few) and then hostess Charla Rhines introduced me, asked what new inventions I was working on (I mentioned Drainbuster and

💡 LONDON AIRE HOSIERY

"Guaranteed to never run"

PROBLEM: *Nylons that run.*

Most people think of me as a kitchen-gadget guy, but in the 1960s I was also the nylon guy. More than half of Ronco's sales in the late 1960s—some 58 percent, in fact—came from London Aire Hosiery. I know a lot of people probably still remember the commercial we did, where we showed how a pair of ordinary hosiery would run badly after we cut them in half with scissors. I compared them to a cut pair of my London Aire hosiery—they were sliced in half, but they didn't run. Then I topped it off by using a scouring pad, a lit cigarette, and a nail file—instruments of torture to show that no matter what, London Aire never ran.

•

Hosiery was a great product because it had mass appeal. Every woman used nylons and all women had trouble with their hosiery running. The product was a low-cost item and no research and development had to go into it. That work was done by the hosiery manufacturers.

•

This project was pure marketing. We didn't have the wherewithal or creativeness at the time to make machinery that would, in fact, create this product, but the mills in North Carolina were already making nylons. We just contracted with them to make the double-locked-stitch hose.

•

An old friend from the fair days, Diane Golding, got us into the nylon hosiery business. While visiting her home in England she passed a marketplace and noticed someone demonstrating nonrun hosiery. She came back to the U.S., had some nylons made for us, and performed a demonstration using a home movie camera. She showed the film to my partner Mel Korey and me, but neither of us really had a feeling for the product. We showed the film to a bunch of gals who worked for us and their response was different, immediate, and unanimous: "Where can we get some?"

●

So now we were in the nylon hosiery business. Since Diane was from England, we called it London Aire. What does London have to do with stockings? What does London Fog have to do with raincoats? It sounds nice. Spend enough money on advertising, and you can make the name work. I didn't particularly know that then, but I certainly know it now.

●

"Longer wear from London Aire . . . Guaranteed in writing not to run!"

Doorsaver), and then we went right into the pitch for the Food Dehydrator.

I didn't have to write an actual script because, remember, I had been selling the Food Dehydrators at the fairs. My demonstration on the infomercial wasn't that much different from the one at the fairs, except that I had someone up there with me who knew nothing about the machine, and posed a lot of important questions the consumer would ask.

Why did I choose the dehydrator for the first infomercial?

There was a great interest in the late 1980s in healthy

foods. Foods without additives and preservatives. The outdoors market was getting big, labeling laws were in the news. And here's this food dehydrator. Make soup mixes without salt, or dried apples and banana chips that aren't loaded with cholesterol-boosting coconut oil.

So I had a health product. One that was made in the USA. One with a high perceived value. Other food dehydrators were selling for anywhere from $70 to $200. I could sell mine for $60 and make it work. So it was the perfect product at the right time. TV infomercial time was very inexpensive then. In the early days of TV if you had an average product with an average commercial you could become rich. The same thing applied to the infomercial business in 1991, except that now you could become even richer.

My 800 phone lines were burning. More money than I could ever dream about was coming through the telephones. And for the first time in my life I knew every morning exactly how much money I had made the day before, because people dialed my toll-free lines, as well as 1-800-43-RONCO, paid with a credit card, and everything was computerized. I had a readout of my sales figures every morning. And unlike the old days, I didn't have to wait six months for the retailers to pay for the product. I was getting paid instantly. What a way to make money!

And, P.S., I still kept my association with Fingerhut, even without USA Direct. I suggested that they take my infomercial and buy their own TV airtime and my product. This was exactly the kind of deal my father had made, where several individuals bought his product and got to use my TV commercial. Instead of calling 1-800-43-RONCO, you called 1-800-FingerH. I sold product and was happy; Fingerhut made money on the dehydrator and they were happy. Additionally, Fingerhut eventually went into the infomercial business, resurrecting USA Direct with an infomercial for a little-known Texas diet guru, a woman who had shed more than

150 pounds and went on to tell the world about it. Her name: Susan Powter. Success breeds success.

My success in infomercials only confirmed my lifelong hunch that, given enough time in my sales pitch, I could sell more product than ever before. If I'm on QVC and get twelve minutes, I do just fair. With fifteen minutes I do great and at twenty minutes it's sensational. It's not much different in infomercials. You transfer from a one-minute commercial to a twenty-eight-minute-and-thirty-second infomercial, and sales will be just phenomenal. When I was working at Woolworth's, I had to make my pitches fast because customers were on their lunch hour and had to get back to work. Imagine how much more product I could have sold had I had the time to really sell. The infomercial is the best sales presentation ever invented for television, because you can speak slowly and really get your point across. The more time you have to do the job, the greater and more effective the presentation will be.

CHAPTER **1 2**

GLH

So there I was, making a mint on the Food Dehydrator with the infomercial. Naturally, with all that money coming in, and all those new, satisfied Ronco customers, the pressure was on to come up with another product.

Some people think you go into a little room, put up a DO NOT DISTURB sign, and work day in and day out until you come up with an idea. That's not how it happens. With something like the Inside-the-Shell Egg Scrambler it can come out of a casual comment about how much I hate slimy egg whites. "I wish there was some way to get rid of them." Or with Mr. Microphone it could be watching someone on TV singing from a wireless mike, and thinking about what a great idea it would be to make a mass market item out of that device. Or, as was the case with GLH, someone can just walk into your life and drop it on your lap.

For GLH that person was Bernice Altschult, the former owner of a popular Los Angeles restaurant called Carlos n' Charlie's. She saw a demonstration in L.A. of a hair spray that covers bald spots and begged me to look at it. For three months she was after me, but I kept turning her down. Why would I want to waste my time with a hair product that couldn't conceivably work? I had just come out with my most successful product, after thirty-five years in the business, and it, like most of my early ones, was for the kitchen. With the kind of acceptance I was getting for the Food Dehydrator, I wanted the next one to be another product for the kitchen.

But Bernice persisted and found a way to get to me. She set up a bogus business meeting with some associates, unbeknownst to me. They mentioned that they were involved with a new hair product and asked me to look at it. I couldn't say no if I wanted to sell them some of my product.

Four days later my designer, Alan Backus, and I went to meet with them in Los Angeles. When it comes to technical know-how, patents, and design, Alan is the master. When I look at new products, I always bring him with me.

We went to see a man in Los Angeles who shall remain nameless. He was from Europe and from the looks of his layout, it seemed that he was in the cosmetics business. He welcomed us in, sat us down, and just like I've done a million times on TV, the man sprayed the product on my bald spot. His spray wasn't as developed as mine is now, but the concept of spraying something on your hair or bald spot was a great concept. I recognized that right away. My reluctance to get involved ended the moment I looked at myself in the mirror and realized what a huge potential market there could be out there.

On the spot I told the man that we had a deal, fifty-fifty, but that we had to perfect the product. He accepted our terms and informed us that his spray was a family product made in Australia. I didn't like that. I prefer to make my products here. Why go all the way down there, deal with shipping, tariffs, delays, duty, and all those other problems? We can produce aerosol sprays here as cheaply as anywhere

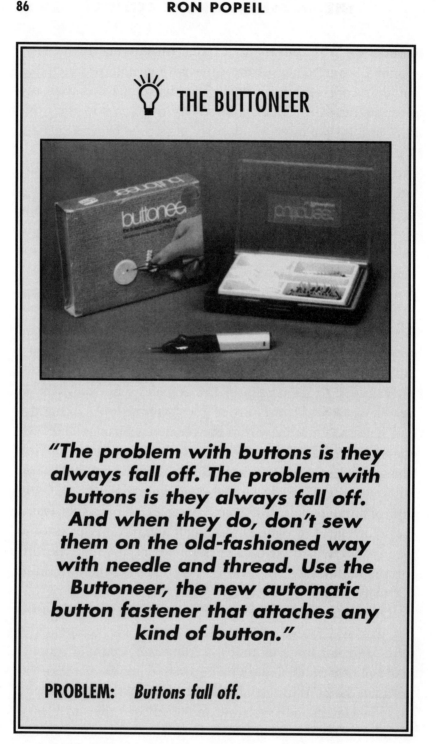

💡 THE BUTTONEER

"The problem with buttons is they always fall off. The problem with buttons is they always fall off. And when they do, don't sew them on the old-fashioned way with needle and thread. Use the Buttoneer, the new automatic button fastener that attaches any kind of button."

PROBLEM: *Buttons fall off.*

Everybody remembers that ad line. I used the phrase *The problem with buttons is they always fall off* twice because I thought that it would make a bigger impact and the consumer would remember it. And it certainly worked.

•

The Buttoneer was made by Dennison Manufacturing of Framingham, Massachusetts, the company that was known for making those little price tags with the plastic T that you always snip off pants and shirts when you bring them home from the store.

•

They had bombed at retail with the Buttoneer. So they came to me. "Ron, we need your help," they said. "We've got this great product, and we don't know what to do with it to make it successful. We've tried everything. Can you do anything with it?"

•

I thought the product was a winner, just marketed poorly. Dennison originally distributed the Buttoneer to stores, using a Christmas-themed Scrooge and Tiny Tim spot that didn't work. What did Scrooge and Tiny Tim have to do with buttons falling off?

•

I offered to begin with a Mother's Day test, and then, if it worked, give the company a firm commitment. I came up with an ad that didn't try to be cute, but instead just explained the problem and my solution, head on. The problem with buttons is that they always fall off. Not anymore. Not if you buy my new amazing product!

•

Dennison had marketed the product for $6.95. I lowered it to $4.99. They sold 20,000 over Christmas. We sold 200,000. Needless to say, the Mother's Day test was so successful that we ordered 600,000 for the following Christmas, and we had a more than 90-percent sell-through.

•

We also made a great deal. They said that in order to get exclusive rights to the product, we would have to buy X numbers of pieces every year. I put into the contract that if we bought more than the X pieces, that additional number could be applied to future years, in terms of the exclusivity clause.

•

The excess quantity I ordered in those early years covered me for an additional four or five years where I didn't have to order any product in order to maintain the exclusive rights.

•

In essence, if they asked me to buy 100,000 pieces the first year, and I wanted to buy 600,000, I'd have the rights for six years, but I wouldn't have to buy any product for the next five years.

•

That has great value because if you spend a lot on advertising and you make the product successful in that year, but you sell fewer than 1,000 pieces the following year, you could lose all your rights and the benefits of the TV ad.

•

This is what I did with Dennison. We ordered the minimum, and the Buttoneer took off after the commercial went on the air. We kept buying and buying, not realizing that by purchasing these excessive quantities, we were protecting ourselves for years to come.

•

"Repair upholstery, pleat draperies, attach appliqués, ribbons, decorate toys, dolls . . . it's the Buttoneer!"

else in the world. We've got the machinery and the know-how.

I told that to the guy and also said that I needed the existing formula as a base to make my job easier, so that Alan could refine it. He agreed to all.

A month passed by, and I asked Alan for a progress report. There was no news, because the guy had refused to give Alan the formula. "He says it's a family trade secret."

Well, this didn't make any sense. Why would the guy want to do a deal with me? If he wanted my participation, my talents, my infomercial, my sales expertise, he would have to give me the formula. Something didn't sound right.

Alan agreed and pointed out that the cans we saw in his office had no labels on them. Wasn't that kind of strange? "I think the man is buying the product from someone else and he's lying to us about him being the owner."

So what should we do? "I'm going on vacation next week, and I know the product comes from Australia. Book two tickets Down Under. We're flying to Sydney."

When we got to Sydney, the first thing we did was check all the stores and beauty salons in the city. I went to one department store, and asked the clerk at the cosmetics section whether he had heard of the guy from L.A. He had, and he didn't have good things to say about him.

"Have you ever heard of a product that you spray over bald spots?"

The answer was no. Nobody had heard of the product. But they all knew the guy we were asking about. And his reputation wasn't good.

Alan left to call a friend of his in Sydney. When he came back, he said the friend had heard of the man and was familiar with the product, and that the product had been invented in the late 1970s by two men. Alan got their names.

We went to visit the first man and discovered that he had a machine in his basement, where he made the product and sold it to local drugstores. The other guy, he told us, lived in Melbourne, but they'd split and had stopped speaking to each other. The products were different from each other—although similar in that they both used a spray to cover bald spots. I cut a deal with the guy in Sydney right there. I gave him $10,000 in American funds for American rights, as well as a piece of my action.

Even though he had what I thought was an inferior product to the one I would market, I wanted to cut a deal. That way, we were protected, and if we were successful, he wouldn't market his product in the United States.

Then we jumped on a plane to Melbourne and found the other guy. I cut the same deal with him. Both men told us they knew the guy from L.A. and said he had totally fabricated the story about the hair product being in his family.

Obviously we weren't going to do business with the man. Had he told me he was buying the product from outside sources, it would have been no problem. I would have made him part of the deal. But I felt it was right to cut him out because he had come to me and outright lied. Later he threatened to sue me but never did, because we didn't have a contract.

So I came back with two different formulas and two contracts with the Australians, who are as happy as larks because they get money from me every year and don't have to work for it. It's like a windfall for them. (Bernice also gets a royalty every month for introducing me to the product. She didn't know the guy was lying.)

Alan and I worked on developing a better formula, which, when we were finished, was just as they say in the infomercials: "Amazing." How was it different from the Australian versions? When you put their formula on your hair, it didn't look real; ours does.

We produced a second *Incredible Inventions* infomercial, this time at a cost of $75,000. And I became a media star because of the novelty of the product. I did *20/20, Prime Time Live, CBS Evening News* with Dan Rather and Connie

Chung, *Good Morning America*, NBC *Nightly News* with Tom Brokaw, *The Maury Povich Show*, *The Joan Rivers Show*, and countless newspaper interviews, including a cover story in *USA Today*, all because people got a kick out of watching a truly incredible invention work, and a salesman who never gave up. On the *CBS Evening News* I was called "a master, a pioneer, the king of the infomercial, a gadget savant." On *20/20* they said I was a "television visionary, the man who turned the hard sell into a blunt instrument, the granddaddy of TV hucksters."

I'll accept the compliments.

GLH really is an innovative and unique product. No one had ever seen anything like it before, which is why I think the media had so much fun with it. It *does* make people look younger. It solves a lot of emotional problems that men have today because of bald spots that make them look older, as well as those of women who have thinning-hair problems. When you look in the mirror and see what appears to be hair and you look ten or fifteen years younger, you say, "Whoa!" People get really excited about it. We sold 900,000 cans in one year. We made millions. All thanks to my friend Bernice and a trip to Australia.

As I say, sometimes these things just fall into your lap.

What I learned in this situation is that persistence pays off and you've got to move fast when competition is breathing down your neck. After I realized that the first man we'd started to deal with wasn't telling us the truth, Alan and I were on a plane to Australia. Once there, we didn't give up until we got the necessary information that led us to the two original inventors, and then we moved really quickly. We went straight to the source and then got the product out in ninety days. I didn't have the luxury to wait for two years to get the product, knowing that the other guy was also out there. I had to move quickly. And it paid off.

PART II

Inventing and

Marketing

If a man write a better book, preach a better sermon, or make a better mouse-trap than his neighbor, tho' he build his house in the woods, the world will make a beaten path to his door.
—Ralph Waldo Emerson

CHAPTER 13

Problems and Solutions

In this section of the book I'm going to tell you how to take your inventions, turn them into successful products, and sell them. If you're not an inventor, I'll tell you how to take an existing product and market it.

Either way, there are five steps you'll follow in most instances:

1. *Find or develop a product.*
2. *Test it among your friends, family, and co-workers to see if it really works and whether there's sufficient interest.*
3. *Find a designer/engineer to make a prototype for you. Then locate a manufacturer, someone who can produce your product for a fair price, one that allows you to make money.*
4. *File for a patent to protect your product and copyright it.*
5. *Package the product, price it, and bring it to market, either via retail, TV marketing, or both.*

I have two simple rules that all my products must abide by. **No. 1: It has to be needed by lots of people.** For example, everyone has problems with buttons falling off at one point or another. The average consumer eats pasta three times a week—not only here in the U.S., but worldwide. Pasta is truly a mass market food product.

Rule No. 2: The product has to solve a problem. *The problem with buttons is they always fall off.* So get the Buttoneer. *Hate preservatives and chemicals in soup mixes and dried foods?* Try the Ronco Electric Food Dehydrator. *Wish you didn't have that pesky bald spot on the back of your head?* Buy a can of GLH: Great Looking Hair, spray it over the spot, and watch it disappear like magic.

What I always do on TV, and on the product packaging itself, is make my customer aware of the problem and how my product offers the solution.

Most of my successful products have been kitchen products. Reason? They're the true definition of mass market. If you're in the product inventing business, *the first question you have to ask yourself is how big will your audience be?*

Everybody has a kitchen, whether they live in apartments, houses, motor homes, or wherever, and everybody experiences problems in the kitchen. Smells . . . messes . . . splattering grease when frying foods . . . dull knives. We attempt to develop products that solve an everyday problem rather than addressing a problem that comes up only once in a while.

Since kitchen items have always made great products over the years, I usually design something that's going to save the consumer time and money and something that's easier to use. Remember, kitchen items make great gifts!

You can spend a lot of money on television advertising to make yourself a celebrity, and you can feel really good about all the attention you get, but sometimes you have to wonder whether the credit is really due. When I talk about my products, I always strive to say they are items that I either invented or marketed. Some of them were created by my father, others by associates I've worked with over the years. Many of them I did invent. But people give me more credit than is really due me. I would love to have been the inventor of truly life-changing products like the safety razor, zipper, or Velcro. Now, those are *real* inventions. I look at my products as innovations. They certainly weren't in the same class as great inventions.

Brainstorming

Where do I get my ideas for products?

First of all, I travel a lot. The Germans and Japanese are great innovators. I love to go over there and see what's working and whether that kind of product might be utilized in this country. The Germans are very creative in both function and design; the Japanese produce quality products that are extremely innovative.

In addition to looking for product ideas abroad, I also spend a lot of time in the U.S.A. cruising department stores, variety stores, fairs, and home shows. While people are shopping for clothes, I'm in the housewares departments thinking up new concepts. If I'm on a cruise ship, when the boat docks, I'm off and onto the island, looking at stores and seeing what they're selling. You should do that too. You'd be

💡 THE RONCO SMOKELESS ASHTRAY

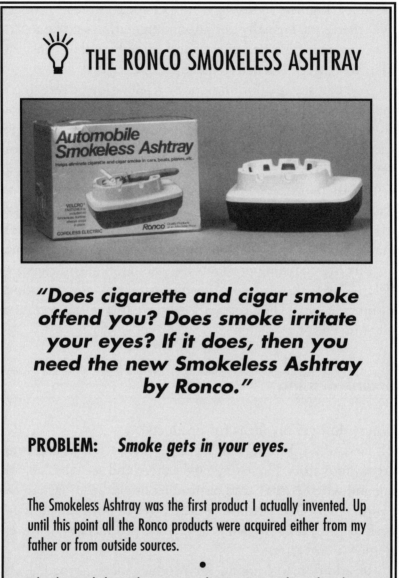

"Does cigarette and cigar smoke offend you? Does smoke irritate your eyes? If it does, then you need the new Smokeless Ashtray by Ronco."

PROBLEM: *Smoke gets in your eyes.*

The Smokeless Ashtray was the first product I actually invented. Up until this point all the Ronco products were acquired either from my father or from outside sources.

•

Why the Smokeless Ashtray? A simple reason. I've always hated cigarette and cigar smoke. And this was back in 1974. We found out later that secondhand smoke is hazardous to your health, but we didn't know it then. Our product really came into its own a few years later when documentation proved secondhand smoke is harmful.

•

The idea of the Smokless Ashtray was that when the consumer would put his cigarette in the ashtray, the smoke would be sucked into it and be absorbed by a filtering system.

•

How did I know where to begin on the design? Let's face it. My father was a manufacturer. I knew that plastic parts were made by a molder. I was certainly aware of that. What I wasn't aware of was what kind of materials you could use to put a burning cigarette in and not have it melt, or disintegrate and go up in flames.

•

I worked with Alan Backus on designing the ashtray. I found Alan through a California research and development company. At this time I was commuting a lot between Chicago and California, because the West Coast is where trends begin. I brought my smokeless-ashtray idea to Alan's R & D company, and six months later, Alan was working for me exclusively.

•

The Smokeless Ashtray did very well and we came up with a line-extension, a portable unit for the car. This way, since the retail store was carrying one unit, we could sell two, side by side. Then we converted the battery-operated unit to electric, so the consumer could buy either one. Many people didn't like having to throw in new batteries all the time; others preferred the battery-operated unit because they could bring it into their cars, boats, even airplanes.

•

What was it like having a hit that I created, as opposed to someone else? No difference. Success is success. We made so much money with the Veg-O-Matic and Spray Gun and Chop-O-Matic, and I had been making so much money all my life on live demonstrations, that I

> never really got a chance to enjoy the products when they were successful. I was always looking ahead to the next one.
>
> •
>
> *"The Smokeless Ashtray. Helps clear the air you breathe. If you smoke, buy one and be considerate of those who don't smoke. If you don't smoke, buy one for those who do. Buy two or three. They really do make great Christmas gifts. And they're only $9.98."*

surprised what you can learn when you research from this angle.

How do I know what the consumer needs? A lot of it is just plain common sense. When I invented the Ronco Smokeless Ashtray in 1974, the antismoking movement was just taking off. People were becoming quite vocal about their annoyance with cigarette smoke. Wouldn't it be nice to have an ashtray with no smoke coming out of it?

There again, I began with the problem. Bothersome cigarette smoke. And I came up with a solution: an ashtray that collected smoke into a filter, so it wouldn't bother others.

Provide a solution to a problem with your product and people will want to buy it.

And what are some of my innovations?

Let's look at the Food Dehydrator. The idea of drying food has been around for hundreds of years. We know the process of drying food is simple: you just have to find a way to extract the moisture. I used convection air flow to move warm air around the food, with openings to allow moisture to escape. It is a well-designed product, big enough to do a sizable job but small enough so that it doesn't take up too much space in the kitchen.

The Ronco Smokeless Ashtray, as I say, was both a solution to the problem and an innovation. I was one of the first to market an ashtray that took smoke particles out of the air with the use of an activated charcoal filter system. My sequel, the Ronco CleanAire Machine, was also innovative. The ashtray collected smoke from a cigarette or cigar; the CleanAire Machine got rid of lots of pollutants—pollen, dust, and odors as well as smoke. I had the benefit of the razor blade business with both of these products, because the filters had to be periodically replaced.

When I invent a product, I don't sit down in a little room and just play with these widgets until I can get them to work. I bring in a team of people who assist me in the development. But understand that developing and marketing a product are like left and right feet. They both must work perfectly for a product to succeed. You could have a great invention, but if you haven't marketed it properly, you've got a big flop.

Americans seem fascinated by inventors. We're celebrities, folk heroes, the common man (or woman) who has made good. Being an inventor (even if you're really an innovator) seems to give you credibility. What's even better is if you can invent, innovate, and market. The combination of the three is sure to make you a media celebrity.

To me, marketing is the most fun and the most rewarding. You can invent a product, but unless you're the guy who's actually selling it, and watching the customers buy, you don't reap the rewards of instant gratification. Sales to me is the equivalent of applause for the actor. So is customer feedback. When someone says to you, "I love your pasta machine and use it every day," and you know that you were the one who made the decisions to create the product and you solved some overwhelming problems in getting it out there, you feel awfully good.

What is marketing? Most think of it purely as selling, especially using advertising, but there's actually much more to the art of marketing. Beyond promoting or trading one's wares, marketing is also the simple act of getting your product to the consumer.

Some of the greatest marketers of all time, including P. T. Barnum, Procter and Gamble, Henry Ford, Louis B. Mayer, and Stephen Wynn, were successful because they marketed things a better way, not just to give people what they want, but also to give them what these marketers want them to think they want.

"The successful showman," wrote P. T. Barnum, "must have a decided taste for catering for the public; prominent perceptive facilities; tact; a thorough knowledge of human nature; great suavity and plenty of 'soft soap.' "

It's not that different today. Just substitute the word *marketer* for *showman* (although I believe both are the same).

You need to know what people are interested in, what they'll spend money for, and be great at getting the word out in a way that makes people want to buy what you have to sell.

What do consumers want today? A quality product at a fair price, and of course, a money-back guarantee. Something that's easy to understand. If it's too difficult to make work, or too complicated, they'll just send it back. So make it simple.

Who is my customer? Everybody. I like to sell mass market items that appeal to everyone. Take the old TV ad I did for the Ronco Bottle and Jar Cutter. "A great hobby for Dad, craft for the kids, a wonderful gift for Mom." Or the Pocket Fisherman, "fishing fun for the whole family." Your product shouldn't be a niche item. You won't make any money that way. It should appeal to everyone.

What Does It Do?

If you don't know what your product does, you'll never be able to sell it. What does my Food Dehydrator do? It makes dried foods. It also saves money and helps make healthier foods for the consumer. If you're an outdoors person, you can make inexpensive dried foods and take them with you in your backpack. If you're a gardener, here's a way to save some of your vegetables for soup mixes instead of canning your excess goods.

So what does it do? The Food Dehydrator saves you money, makes healthy food, and provides you with a lot of fun in your kitchen. GLH: it will make you look younger. My Pasta Machine makes fresh pasta. It's fun, easy to use, and will save you money. The Buttoneer: it will replace your buttons fast, the new way, without using a needle and thread.

Gifts

The next thing to remember about your product is that it *has to be able to be positioned as a gift*. Everyone is looking for a new gift to give someone. We're a gift-giving society. People laugh at the commercialization of the Christmas selling season, but the fact is, that's when the retail stores make their money. Without Christmas every major retailer today would be bankrupt.

When I design a product, I always think about its gift-giving potential. If you're introducing a product, don't put it in the store in July, because there's not much foot traffic. Fewer people come into the stores to buy in the summer, and when they do, their interest usually is for back-to-school clothes for their kids. Just look at the annual reports of the retailers, and you'll see that most business is done in the fourth quarter.

I've always tried to develop unique products, items that you don't already own. That says to me the market is there. If it's priced right, it's positioned to make a good gift. And if it's easy to use, it will probably sell.

The one thing people in Ottumwa, Iowa, and New York City share in common is this: Their buying habits may be different, but they still have to buy gifts for Christmas, Mother's Day, Father's Day, birthdays, weddings, showers, and so on. We live in a gift-giving society. *Don't forget that.*

How to Get Your Own Ideas

A new product could be as simple as your own invention or simply a repackaging and updating of an old concept. Ideas for your future products are out there, everywhere, in abundant supply. It's just a matter of looking for them.

How do I do it? I look for problems to solve in the home, automobile, and personal-care categories—areas where the consumer can relate to problems that she or he encounters on a frequent basis. The next thing I do is my homework. I look into what is already in the U.S. and foreign marketplace. The product you may be looking for may exist overseas but has never come to the U.S., as evidenced by GLH (Australia) or Miracle Brush (Japan). There are also products out there that have never been marketed that may solve the problem you're trying to solve. You must really educate yourself about what's out there in association with the problem.

The first place to look is domestic and foreign store shelves. Then you want to know what patents have been issued in that category. You can get a lot of great ideas from libraries. I buy lots of products—everything related to the product I'm attempting to invent or innovate. After I've done my research, I'm ready to sit down with my development team and review what's been done, how we can take advantage of it, and what we can do to create the better mousetrap.

I usually find great ideas in stores, but they're also at fairs and conventions and on television. I'm always looking.

Going through old patents can provide you with some great ideas. Many past products may be ready for a comeback. Perhaps by just giving them a new twist or modern application, you can hit a real winner. We found the concept for the Inside-the-Shell Egg Scrambler from an old patent. The old product used a crank to make it work. It was bulky and not practical for use in an average kitchen. We redesigned it so it was small, added electricity, and thus modernized an old product with new technology and it was readily accepted by consumers.

Overall, gut feeling and plain common sense should steer you down the right path.

Also investigate trade journals. There's a publication for almost every kind of business out there (*Pizza Today, Electronic Retailing, The Frozen Food Executive, Advertising Age,* and even *Funeral Director)* and many are available at the library. They're great sources of material, with information about people like you and their products, as well as upcoming industry events that you might want to consider attending. If nothing else, you'll get a good feel for how competitors price their products and how they present their products to store buyers. The trade magazines that I read to keep up with my industry are *HomeWorld, Housewares Executive, HFD (Home Furnishings Daily), Direct Response TV Magazine, Jordan Whitney's Television Merchandiser,* and *Steven Dworman's Infomercial Marketing Report.*

Patent Research

It's amazing how many ideas you can pick up just from studying past and present patents. I'm convinced that there have been many products over the years that were invented just this way (after studying expired patents). With the technology today to enhance some of those old inventions, you could end up with a successful consumer product for mass marketing.

If you like a particular category, go to the library and research that area. For instance, if you were interested in inventing, say, an egg scrambler machine, look up the category of egg machines. You'll come up with a gadzillion ideas of past inventions—some have expired, some have not. Either way, you'll get some great ideas on how to proceed.

Brainstorming Exercises

Here are some other tools to help lead you to new products:

- **Apply new technology:** Ronco's RollerMeasure wasn't the first tape measurer, but it did take advantage of new technology—digital readouts, then found in calculators and watches. We introduced a tape measurer that used a wheel to measure walls, ceilings, and around corners and solved the problem of adding up inches in your brain, by simply providing the solution of a digital readout.
- **Time Savers:** Convenience is what consumers are after in the 1990s. How can they save time? With the Pasta Machine they can not only save money but they can make and produce fresh homemade pasta in two minutes. A short spray of GLH onto a bald spot is a lot

cheaper and faster than getting a hair weave. The Buttoneer put buttons back on without having to go through the bother of sewing.

Prepared baby food was invented in the 1920s by Dan Gerber when he learned how much his wife hated the task of straining adult foods for their baby. How many products can you come up with that can save people time and money?

- **Improve an Existing Product:** Find something that doesn't work well (as I did with other pasta machines), analyze what went wrong with it, and fix it. IBM changed the face of the typewriter industry in the 1960s when it introduced interchangeable typefaces. Most people were happy with playing vinyl albums on their turntables and cassettes on their tape decks until the compact disc was introduced in the 1980s. The CD was capable of reproducing music without the bothersome scratches, warps, and nicks of vinyl. Additionally, you never had to get up and turn the CD over to hear another side. And if all that wasn't enough—the CD also sounded a lot better than the LP. Result: Vinyl records disappeared from record stores.
- **Be from Mars:** Look at American life with the eyes of an outsider. Pretend that you've just come to America from another planet, and you're seeing everything in your home for the first time. Does everything work the way it should? Could there be a better way of doing something?
- **Study Trends:** There is no better way to stay atop of the ever-changing desires of the American consumer than to keep track of the latest trends and fads. The best way to do that is by looking at what's going on and by reading as much different information as you can. The local newspaper is important and there're hundreds of magazines out there directed to different segments of our society. Look at them closely as well.

You may hate what network television has to offer, but familiarize yourself with the top 20—watch the trendiest and highest-rated shows at least once. What you're seeing is American pop culture on display, for thirty minutes every week. What the characters talk about is usually what America is talking about.

And speaking of America, people live at the mall. Walk through these urban and suburban subcultures as often as you can, and study the stores. Look at what's for sale, what's being offered, what people are buying, and at what price. You may develop a product that improves on what is out there and one you could bring to the marketplace for much less money.

Study trends and keep up on major social changes on both the national and personal level. Look at what's happening in this country. The health movement is what convinced me to come out with my Food Dehydrator. People are demanding fewer preservatives and additives, and I thought they'd appreciate a product that would help them make healthier food. I was right.

Let's examine other current topics like the increase in single-parent households (maybe that's why you see so many easy-to-cook frozen foods at the market), the baby boom (upscale baby goods), the concern with the environment (the Smokeless Ashtray!), to mention a few.

Examine your own life. What recent changes have occurred? If things are happening to you and your friends, chances are the same things are going on with others as well. What new products do those changes suggest?

Design

I realized a long time ago that I'm not an expert in every area. That's why I work with professionals to assist me in the

creation and marketing of my products. I do know what consumers like, and how to market a product, but I know very
little about engineering, about motors, and how things work
internally. So I bring in professionals to work with me and
have always been fortunate enough to surround myself with
people who I always felt were a lot smarter.

My designer/engineer is Alan Backus, whom I have been
working with exclusively for the last fifteen years on the design of my products. I met him after I took my concept for
the Smokeless Ashtray to a research and development firm
in Los Angeles. Alan worked for the firm and did such a
great job on my invention that I hired him away to work for
me.

We begin the process with a conversation. I usually tell
Alan what function I want for the product and what size and
shape I think it should be. Then he goes off and sketches
ideas. I then look at four or five different ideas before selecting something for the prototype.

Prototypes

Making a prototype is essential. Having a good model of
your invention will solidify your thinking and help in everything from market research to selling your idea.

There are three different kinds of prototypes:

- **A Working Model** is fully functional and strong
  enough to withstand the testing process, but may not use
  the same materials as the final version. This is what we
  start off with.
- **A Preproduction Model** uses the same type of tooling
  as the final version will use in production, but it might dif-
  fer in a few key areas.

💡 THE RONCO CLEANAIRE MACHINE

"The Antipollution Machine"

PROBLEM: *Smoke still gets in your eyes.*

At this point in the late 1970s the Ronco CleanAire Machine was probably the best-quality product I had been involved with. People who had respiratory problems, possibly because of cigar or cigarette smoke, or just didn't like kitchen or bathroom odors (and who does?), really loved my new product.

•

Mine wasn't the only company that created a small home air-filtering machine, but I made sure that mine was the best. I had reached a point in my life where quality was paramount to me, and when I made my commercial, I challenged my competition by using seven of theirs against one of mine, saying my machine would outperform all seven of them. (The retail prices of our products were similar.)

•

My TV commercial was challenged by consumer advocate David Horowitz on his old TV show *Fight Back*. But on his show, after he tested, he agreed that my one machine outperformed all seven of the competition. The reason? Because we had a better filter, motor combination, and design. It's that simple.

•

In the TV ad we showed smoke-filled offices and family rooms with so much cloudy smoke that you couldn't see people. It wasn't that much different a sales pitch from the Smokeless Ashtray, but on a larger scale. Since people at the time were really into the quality of the air they were breathing, we were able to sell hundreds of thousands of ashtrays. So obviously we knew we could sell CleanAire Machines too.

•

"Now any room can have fresher, cleaner air."

- **The Production Model** is the exact replica of what you plan on selling in the stores, using the same materials, sizes, colors, and manufacturing processes. This is your final version.

As with everything else in the world, you can make the prototype yourself or pay someone else to do it. I turn to my expert, Alan Backus, because he's so good at it, while I can't draw a straight line. For companies that specialize in making prototypes and models, look in the Yellow Pages, under "Product Designers," "Designers-Industrial," and "Inventors."

There are also a lot of design schools. You might consider taking your idea to a design school. One of the students might be able to help you put the product together. Sometimes they know many shortcuts to building inexpensive functioning models. (That, of course, is after you've done your homework and have protected your idea, something I'll get into in Chapter 15).

Testing

Once we have the prototype, we test and test and test. If it's a kitchen product, we'd like it to be dishwasher safe, because that's an important selling tool. All types of products have to be able to withstand the drop test. Before the QVC home shopping channel will accept a product to sell, it has to still be intact after being dropped six feet! The more durable the product, the better material you use, the greater cost it will have.

Cost is always a factor. At the same time, you don't want to build a product the consumer will take home, use a couple of times, and then have it break. The product will either be returned or stuck in the closet. You need good word of mouth and repeat business if you're going to stick around.

You'll want to test your product to iron out the kinks now—and to be sure whether there really is a market for your item before you start putting out the dollars for production and marketing. If you believe your product is marketable, you need more to go on than just your gut feeling. You need to do a little research.

I heard of a guy who came up with a great new kind of cat food. Since cat food, like cosmetics, comes down to marketing, the man was convinced he had a winner. He had his ad agency put out terrific ads and an eye-catching package. They did such a good job for him, he moved 2,000 cases of cat food the first week. But never again. Reason? He had neglected to test his concoction with his most important consumer—cats! And they hated what he had to sell.

Before you get second opinions on your product, thoroughly research your competition. You should know everything that came out beforehand and what happened to it. You need to buy every kind of similar product that you possibly can and look at it. I decided to bring out my Pasta Machine only after I looked at my competitors and found that their machines were overpriced, didn't do the job very well, and used inferior materials in construction.

Buy all the competing products you can find and examine them carefully. Try to understand the good and bad, and then try to come out with something that is much better. You can take your competitors' merchandise back to wherever they came from, and get your money back! You've got very little to lose. To market something too close to someone else's product is just a waste of time. The market can't bear ten people making the same product unless you're the first or second one out there.

Take the Hula Hoop. It was a tremendous product, but no one made any serious money on it because so many people made it. It was nonpatentable. Anybody who made a hose could make a Hula Hoop. You can make big money if you're one of the relatively few or the only one making a product.

After you've conceived your idea, test it on your family and friends. See if they share your enthusiasm. Do they like your product idea, and if so, why? Would they buy it? At what price? When you show it, ask your friends to be brutally honest. Most people will give you a positive reaction because they don't want to hurt your feelings. Insist they tell you the truth. That's the only way you'll know if you have something worth pursuing or not.

If you pass the tests with your friends, keep on going with other demographic groups. Then go back and have them study your prototypes. Ask them hard questions; see what turns them on and off. Use the feedback to perfect your product. And if all of your research findings are negative, realize that perhaps this isn't the product to bring to the market. That decision can save you lots of money and many hours of wasted efforts. Appreciate failures and learn from them. But don't take it personally. Just get back in there and keep trying. Most new products fail. Just like most new TV shows are bombs, few records get into the top 20, and of the 50,000 new books published every year, only a few will become best-sellers. You never know for sure what will click with the public. If more of us did, we'd all be millionaires.

How does a big company like Procter & Gamble go

about testing their products? I understand they begin with hundreds of their own employees, then panels of consumers—hundreds of thousands each year. P & G will introduce the product only if it wins a majority of consumer votes against all major competitors. They have to be convinced that their product is better. For toothpaste or mouthwash, where individual tastes may vary quite a bit, P & G is satisfied with 55 percent approval; for a new toilet paper, however, it has to be 80 percent. Once they're happy with the results, they'll move on to the next phase of testing, easing a product into a market or two gradually and analyzing the sales results. If they're happy with them, then, and only then, will they introduce the product nationally.

I don't believe in wasting a year and a half on consumer testing. That's the advantage of having a small company. I want to get out there now.

But before I start marketing, I do believe in feedback. I like to try it out on people, but I'm not interested in hearing about how great it is. I want to know what's wrong with it. What don't they like? That's how I learn.

But I've never spent a year on testing. For me, speed is number one. I don't want to take so many months out of my life; I want to get out there fast. There are too many people breathing down my neck to find out what my next category or product is. I don't have the luxury of testing a product for a year like P & G. I've got to move quickly so I can capture the marketplace. While others are dreaming, I'm out there.

Here's one way not to test: Don't take your product to a retail buyer for his or her opinion. I can't tell you how many people have come to me with their products and told me how a buyer at such and such store said it was wonderful. Maybe he or she truly felt that way. But more likely the buyer doesn't want to hurt someone's feelings, and rather than tell the inventor the truth, he or she passes it off by saying it's a great idea. Whenever someone tells me that story, and I've heard it literally hundreds of times, I always pose the same question: "How many did he order?" And always, the answer comes up zero.

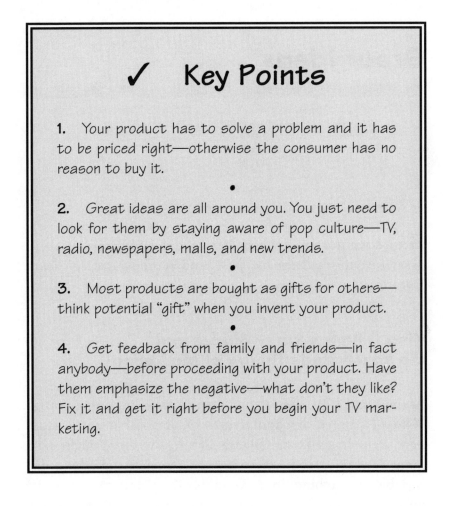

✓ Key Points

1. Your product has to solve a problem and it has to be priced right—otherwise the consumer has no reason to buy it.

•

2. Great ideas are all around you. You just need to look for them by staying aware of pop culture—TV, radio, newspapers, malls, and new trends.

•

3. Most products are bought as gifts for others— think potential "gift" when you invent your product.

•

4. Get feedback from family and friends—in fact anybody—before proceeding with your product. Have them emphasize the negative—what don't they like? Fix it and get it right before you begin your TV marketing.

CHAPTER **14**

Great Ideas

Before we go any farther, let's take a good look at some great inventions from the past, and see how we can learn from them.

King Gillette's Razor Blades and the Razor-Blade Theory of Marketing

In the late 1890s King Gillette was a traveling salesman for William Painter, a manufacturer of disposable bottle stoppers. Painter spoke to Gillette about how there might be a good future for someone who could invent something disposable, something that could be used and then thrown away. The idea was that the customer would always have to come back for more. From that conversation came the idea for the "safety" razor.

At the time, men shaved either with a straight razor or not at all; many men back then had full beards. More than fashion was at stake. The process of shaving one's beard was a very painful if not dangerous exercise. It hurt and nine times out of ten it would result in shaving cuts.

Improvement was definitely called for. Gillette came up with a sharpened steel blade, clamped between plates held together by a screw device that also served as a handle. Enough of the blade would protrude to present a proper edge to the face, but not so much as to easily nick a shaver. Gillette carved a model from a block of wood, and with the help of a machinist, worked on several prototypes to show to prospective investors.

Gillette priced the razors dirt cheap, knowing that if he could hook folks with his new invention, they would come to him again and again for razor blades. In 1904, Gillette's first year of full production, he sold 90,000 razors and a phenomenal 12.4 million blades.

Gillette quickly established a reputation for marketing brilliance by selling "Service Set" shaving kits (3.5 million razors and 36 million blades) to departing servicemen during World War I. When the boys returned, they were confirmed Gillette customers.

Not only was King Gillette a marketing genius, he also revolutionized the way men (and later women) shaved. Not bad.

Edwin Land and the Polaroid: Smart Patents

As an eighteen-year-old undergraduate at Harvard in 1928, Edwin Land experimented with light waves and discovered a method for polarizing light—basically eliminating rays in a light beam unless they were traveling on a single plane, thus reducing glare. Thinking of obvious applications in the auto industry, Land dropped out of school to pursue his invention.

Detroit turned him down flat, so Land turned to sunglasses, where he did big business during World War II with the manufacture of glasses, goggles, and filters. But when the war ended, his sunglass business went down the tubes. He needed another great idea.

In 1943, on vacation in Santa Fe, New Mexico, Land snapped a picture of his three-year-old daughter. When she asked how long it would take before she could see the finished product, Land wondered if it wouldn't be possible to develop and print a photograph inside a camera. He decided to take an existing, popular product, and try to make it better.

After five years of research, in 1947 he introduced the Polaroid Model 95, which produced sepia-toned pictures in sixty seconds. Land brought it to Kodak, but they dismissed his great invention as a toy and turned down the golden opportunity to market the Polaroid.

So Land marketed the camera and film himself, retailing the model at $90. Despite the huge cost his invention was an instant success.

By 1950 he had replaced sepia toned with black and white; color came in 1963 and in 1972 he introduced the SX-70, the first Polaroid to combine a negative and positive print on a single sheet, thereby eliminating the process of peeling off the back of the print after one minute.

Kodak quickly saw the error of its ways and spent years trying to figure out a way to get around Land's patents and into instant photography. In 1976 Kodak finally came up with an "instant" camera. The company thought it had finally come up with an original system that didn't breach any of Polaroid's patents. Land disagreed and sued Kodak for patent infringement, and won, several years later, costing Kodak some hundreds of millions, and forcing the company to get out of the instant photography business.

Land came up with one of the greatest inventions of the

twentieth century, and he got the idea from a simple question from his daughter. He thoroughly patented his idea so nobody could steal it, and like Gillette, he was a master of marketing a product that keeps customers coming back. What good was a Polaroid camera if you didn't have any film?

Whitcomb L. Judson and the Zipper: Just a Great Idea

Before the zipper came along, men fastened their pants with string and buttons and ladies squeezed themselves into long corsets.

Whitcomb Judson thought there had to be a better way. A mechanical engineer, he invented the first zipper (then called the Clasp Locker) in 1891. It's an ingenious little device and it's so simple: one row of hooks and eyes slotting neatly into another row by means of a tab.

Yet it took twenty-two years for Judson to perfect his invention, and another inventor to make the zipper really practical. The zipper had to be produced cheaply, because no one would pay a lot of money for it. So Judson invented a machine to mass-produce his slide-fastener. But it didn't work well.

In 1905, Judson invented a new fastener, the C-Curity, which was easier to manufacture. But traditional clothing firms weren't willing to take it on, so Judson had peddlers try to sell them door to door as novelties.

The zipper finally hit its stride when Judson hired a young engineer, Gideon Sundback, to work for him. Gideon came up with a way to make it more flexible and practical, and machinery to manufacture it cheaply.

The zipper went mainstream in 1918 when another inventor presented to the Army a flying suit he had invented. The Army tested it, and the entire thing fell apart—except for the zipper. A Navy officer happened to see the tests, and Judson's unknown little firm got an order for 10,000 fasteners. (The name "zipper" didn't actually come into being until B. F. Goodrich & Co. put the fasteners into their rubber galoshes and christened them "Zippers.")

Here's a product that took a problem and offered a great solution.

Can't you just hear Whitcomb Judson doing a TV ad for the zipper in the 1970s: "The problem with pants is that it takes too long to put them on. Get pants with the zipper, and be out of the house in a jiffy!"

CHAPTER **15**

Protecting Your Product

"The patent system added the fuel of interest to the fire of genius."
—Abraham Lincoln

There are all sorts of copyrights, trademarks, service marks, trade names, design and function patents you can use to help ensure that a competitor doesn't steal your idea. These will help guard against knockoffs, but the sad inevitability of life is that if you have a hit others will try to copy it. There's no way around it. Still, as we've learned, it pays to protect your properties.

In 1993 the United States Patent and Trademark Office granted a record 109,876 patents. From large corporations and universities to small businesses and individual inventors, everyone seems to be scrambling to patent their ideas. They've been doing that since the birth of this country when George Washington signed the first U.S. patent, back in 1790. It went to a man named Samuel Hopkins of Philadelphia for an improvement in "the making of pot ash and Pearl Ash by a new Apparatus and Process."

Even though millions of patents have been applied for over the years, I don't necessarily believe it needs to be your

💡 MR. MICROPHONE

"Hey, good lookin', I'll be back to pick you up later."

PROBLEM: *There was no problem. For once in my inventing and marketing career, Mr. Microphone was just plain fun . . . and profit.*

Mr. Microphone is easily one of my most fondly remembered products. People seem to associate it with their childhood. If nothing else, I look back at our ad for Mr. Microphone as one of our all-time best.

•

The product was simply a wireless microphone that could broadcast through a frequency on the FM dial. While stores were gobbling up the CleanAire Machine and Buttoneer, I decided to go in a different direction for our next product: the huge music market.

•

Singing or entertaining is very easy to demonstrate, and let's face it, everyone at one time or the other sings in the shower. Millions do it every morning along with their radio, on their way to work.

•

With Mr. Microphone you could make speeches without an amplifier by using any FM radio. It was a great item for kids and parties because everybody could do it together. I had always stayed away from toys, but when I realized the possibilities of broadcasting through the FM band, I saw a huge worldwide market segment.

•

I first came up with the idea for Mr. Microphone when I saw people on TV walking around a stage with a wireless mike. I thought that it would make a great consumer product and started researching the competition. I found a toy that was similar in concept to what would become Mr. Microphone (it also used the FM channel to emit the sound), but it didn't work very well. So, as I always try to do, I went to work to build a better mousetrap.

•

I knew nothing about electronics, but I was able to have the product engineered for me. I worked with engineers and FCC lawyers and a Hong Kong manufacturing firm with expertise in electronic products.

•

The toy I had found wasn't advertised on television, so not a lot of people knew about it. I've done that many times. Many people think of my Pasta Machine as the first one out there even though that's certainly not the case. I'm just the only guy who decided to spend millions of dollars spreading the word about my machine on TV, so people thought I was the pioneer.

•

Besides making the decision to go on TV, I also came up with a great, instantly memorable name, Mr. Microphone, and then went to work to create the ad.

•

It was simply various people, walking, skating, driving, while talking and singing into the Mr. Microphone. My daughter Shannon was one of them. She was sitting in the car next to the guy who said, "Hey, good lookin', I'll be back to pick you up later." I contend it's one of our best commercials from memory lane because it not only had the hard sell but also a lot of entertainment value. It wasn't just the standard sales pitch.

•

We went on to sell over 1 million Mr. Microphones, but the product eventually died off because of knockoffs. Everybody and his brother were making Mr. Microphone clones.

•

But my major knockoff wasn't from my typical competition, it was done by a huge national electronics manufacturer found in virtually every shopping mall in America. They made a product so similar to mine that even I couldn't tell the difference. They put the final nail in Mr. Microphone's coffin.

•

And this retail chain certainly wasn't shy about riding on my coattails. It drove me batty. I had several of my staffers go into fifty of their stores and ask for Mr. Microphone. Ninety percent of the time they were handed their version, with no explanation that it was a different product.

•

> I sued them but lost. The judge wouldn't allow us to present that key piece of evidence. I believe the reason we lost had nothing to do with the merits of the case, but simply that the judge didn't like my lawyers. That case made me lose my faith in the judicial system. Maybe I should have had Robert Shapiro as my lawyer.
>
> •
>
> *"It's practical and great fun for the whole family, and it's only $14.88. Buy two or three, they really make great gifts!"*

first step. The process is costly and time consuming. In most cases it's simply a waste of time and money. Many people wrongly think that getting a patent is a seal of approval or guarantee of protection. The fact is a patent neither guarantees you can build an invention nor does it guarantee you will make any money from it if you do. If someone else has patented another aspect of your product that you can't design around, you may not be able to legally make, use, or sell your product; and if no one wants to buy your product, you may lose money on it.

If you have an idea, the first thing you want to do is protect it in some form, but that doesn't have to be by patent nor does it have to involve a serious expense. For a small fee (currently $10) you can register the date of your invention, for up to two years, with the U.S. Patent and Trademark Office in their "Disclosure Document" program. Just send a complete description of your device, including details of its construction and use, drawings of it, and details of alternative constructions and alternate uses for it, to the U.S. Patent and Trademark Office along with the fee. Call the U.S. Patent and Trademark Office in Washington, D.C., for details. This gives you no protection against being copied, but it protects you in case someone else claims he or she came up with the idea first. In case two people come up with the same idea, or someone copies your idea, patents are held to be valid for the individual who first had the idea and diligently pursued it.

Once you have (or anyone else has) either tried to sell a product using your idea or published your idea, you have one year in the U.S. to apply for a patent. In many cases, however, such a sale or publication in foreign countries ends the possibility of getting foreign patents. That is unless you have already applied for a U.S. patent and received a one-year grace period for foreign filings from the time of your U.S. application date. Consult a patent attorney to be sure.

U.S. patents protect only in the U.S., so if you think your idea has possibilities in the foreign markets, you may be forced to go to a patent attorney and start U.S. and/or foreign applications even before you've marketed in the U.S.

A patent is like an agreement between you and the government issuing the patent. In exchange for you making all the details of your invention public, the government grants you a patent and gives you the exclusive right to make, use, and sell your product for a period of time. Patents can last up to seventeen years in the U.S. Anyone else who wants to make your product must legally get your permission first.

The process of getting a patent is a long, expensive, difficult bureaucratic procedure. It can take three years or even longer. Your costs can be thousands of dollars. And once you have the patent, you are not really protected against knock-offs or unauthorized copies. The only way you can enforce your patents is to bring a lawsuit, and in addition to the costs, there's no way of telling which way the judicial system will go when you're before the judge.

There are some advantages to having a patent, however. It may discourage others from trying to compete and it provides some assurance that others will not claim ownership of your idea. But I still think you can do all of that by simply applying for a patent. I believe that just filing for a patent with the famous phrase *Patent Pending* is just as good in the beginning as having the patent.

In fact in some cases having a patent application may be even better than having a patent. If you have a patent, anyone can read it and possibly design around it. When you have only *Patent Pending* written on your product, what do your competitors design around? They haven't seen your patent. It's pending, not published. Would you invest heavily in product R & D, tooling, inventory, and marketing if tomorrow someone might be issued a patent that might knock your product out of the marketplace? Probably not.

Still, in today's competitive copycat world, there are companies that may copy your product exactly to make one or two years of profit before your patent is issued. You just never know what your competition will do. Damages don't start against a competing infringer until you're issued a patent.

Patents and patent applications, however, do give you something to sell.

Take the case of Advanced Toner Technology (ATT), a small toner cartridge company in Salt Lake City. Two bowlers met in a league, and decided to work together to make a better high-performance toner cartridge. Their cartridge tested well, and they formed a company to market the product. They also consulted patent attorneys who quickly filed a patent application to cover their invention. "Until we had a patent pending on this invention, no one took us seriously," ATT principal Bud Randolph told *Utah Business* magazine.

As I've already stated, you could wait three years or longer for the government to finally come through with your patent. It makes no sense for you to lose valuable marketing time waiting for Washington to come through for you. If your product is successful, having a patent pending will give you at least some protection. If it's a flop, you can abandon the patent application and avoid the remaining patent costs.

How do you apply for a patent?

If you follow my advice about disclosing your invention to the patent office, you're already under way. You should have a clear and complete written description of your invention and how it's constructed and used, along with drawings of it, specifications of alternative constructions and alternative uses for it.

Next, you should research what products have preceded your product. This is done by a look in stores and, more importantly, by a patent search. You could do your own patent search by going to Washington, D.C., but chances are as a first-time searcher you would do an incomplete job and it would be expensive. Better to hire a professional patent search firm.

Most patent attorneys offer patent search services. However, they simply hire specialized patent search firms and tack on a service charge and substantial fee for interpreting the search results. Some invention development firms have a listing under "Patent Search" in the Yellow Pages. Invention development firms are companies that claim to help inventors by promoting their inventions to companies that might market and distribute the new inventions. I'm sure there are a few invention development firms that are reputable, but most seem to take large amounts of your money and produce little results. Try to get a Washington, D.C., Yellow Pages book in your library or from your phone company and look up "Patent Search." Why Washington, D.C.? Because that's where the U.S. Patent and Trademark Public Search Room is (actually Crystal City in Alexandria, Virginia), and consequently that is where most professional patent search firms are.

It generally takes one to three weeks for a patent search

company to complete a search. It may cost from $300 to about $800, depending on the number of prior patents uncovered and the complexity of your invention. Tell the firm you want a search to locate prior art (otherwise known as earlier related patents) in anticipation of your filing a patent application. You may send them part or all of your invention description so they know what to search for. Be sure to mark your invention description "CONFIDENTIAL."

Once you have the results of your patent search, read the patents it uncovers. Pay particular attention to anything that looks close to your invention. Your first concern should be that you don't infringe prior patents that have not yet expired. To determine this, go to the back of each in-force closely related patent and start reading the numbered paragraphs, called "claims," which occur after the bold words *I claim* or *We claim*. If any one of these paragraphs describes your product closely (not necessarily exactly), consult an attorney.

Paragraphs that reference an earlier paragraph, such as by saying, "9) The device as in claim 7 further including . . ." are read as if they were extensions of the numbered paragraph referenced (in this case you would read all of claim 7 and then add to the end of it all the wording of claim 9). If you find a claim paragraph closely describing your product, consult an attorney and limit his or her time to reviewing the specific claim or claims you are not sure whether you infringe. Introducing a new product is tough enough without being sued for patent infringement.

Next, reread entirely the patents uncovered in the search to get a feel for what has already been disclosed to the public, what is still novel, and how they have worded their specification (the invention description that is found in the front part of each patent) and claims (you might want to copy their style).

If you pass all of the above, you're now ready to file a

patent application. To do this, first you must find a good patent attorney. Look in your Yellow Pages under "Patent Attorneys" and interview several firms. I suggest at least three, and keep written notes. No firm should charge you for an interview visit, but confirm this before meeting with them. What you are ideally looking for is a patent attorney with common sense, good communication skills, a knowledge of the law, experience in your product area, experience in writing many patent applications, and preferably one with experience working in the patent office—in that order. Lower rates also don't hurt, providing they're not at the expense of skill.

A good attorney should be able to clearly explain the patent process to you. It's not complicated. The attorney should also be able to give you an estimate of how much he or she will charge for your invention to be put through each stage of the patent application process. Note down these estimates; my experience is that attorneys frequently forget what prices they used to entice you to use their services. If your attorney can't clearly explain what's going on or give you relatively precise cost estimates, find another. I've often found that use of "legalese" and stilted language is a cover for a poor understanding of the subject matter. Common sense and good communications skills are the key thing to look for in your attorney. It will help you work efficiently together and help to persuade the patent office of the validity of your patent application claims.

What can you expect when you apply for a patent? Rejection. It's the patent office's job. Your and your attorney's jobs are to convince the patent office you're entitled to the protection that the law allows.

Many inventors simply give up after hearing a first rejection from the patent office. In all my years of inventing I can recall only once when even one of my patent claims was accepted in the first patent office response. That was on a claim that had twenty-one restricting phrases and extended over more than one full page. In other words, it was a claim that afforded almost no protection because each phrase narrowed or limited the claim.

A patent office rejection is the rule, not the exception. However, they must give you reasons for their turndown. In responding to the patent office you must convince the patent examiner that his or her reasons are not valid (a very hard thing to do), or you must modify your application so the reasons for rejection are no longer relevant. It may require two, three, four, or more communications back and forth between you and the patent office before they accept your application. Don't lose faith—persistence pays, sometimes handsomely.

One other thing: You may receive a communication from the patent office that says "This action is final," or words to similar effect. This usually happens after their second or third response. However, nothing is ever final with the patent office until you choose to make it so. You can file application extensions (called continuations or continuations in part) for a moderate filing fee until the cows come home. Nevertheless, I don't encourage this unless you genuinely feel there has been a miscommunication, or unless you feel you have a new way to convince them that you deserve patent protection.

Next, in a surprising number of cases, expect your attorney, no matter how good he or she is, to do a less than perfect job in writing your application. Why? For two reasons. The first is common sense. Your attorney knows far less about your invention than you do. Better you should write the description of your invention rather than your attorney. Just make the description as clear and complete as you possibly can. Include all the primary uses and constructions as well as any alternate uses and constructions you can think of. Be sure to use (and reference) drawings to illustrate and make your description clearer. Look at the earlier patents uncovered in your search to see how this is done. There are no points deducted here for being too wordy or for bad grammar. But be sure you are clear and complete, or better yet, be overly clear and overly complete. Leave the cleanup to your attorney.

The second reason patent attorneys write less than perfect patent applications has to do with human nature. It's easier to get narrow protection for an idea than broad protection. So, many times attorneys will seek patent protection that is narrow and affords less coverage, but is easy to get. The best way around this is for you to study earlier patents in the invention area and ask your attorney why claims aren't being written to cover any specific areas of your invention you consider unique and useful. Also, think like your competitor and see how easy it would be to design around your claims. If it isn't difficult, then you might try variations that present a bigger challenge. With the proper attitude and persistence you can provide hours of unwelcome entertainment for would-be competitors.

U.S. patents fall into three categories: *Utility* patents, *Design* patents, and *Plant* patents.

- **Utility** patents are the most valuable. They're the kind people usually mean when they speak of patents and what my comments above are most directed to. A utility patent covers the mechanical designs and functions of inventions. In the U.S. these patents have a maximum life of seventeen years.
- **Design** patents cover ornamental or visual aspects of manufactured articles, rather than their structures or utilitarian features. U.S. design patents have a maximum life of fourteen years.
- **Plant** patents, also good for up to seventeen years, protect new kinds of vegetables, flowers, trees, shrubs, and other plants.

The standards for utility patents are meant to be hard to meet. Basically, the invention must be new, useful, and not obvious. What is the government's definition of *new?* It has to do with whether and when the invention was described in print (including earlier patents) or made available for sale. And *usefulness* means the invention actually performs a utilitarian purpose. *Not obvious* means the invention would not be obvious to someone having ordinary skill in the field. For instance, the substitution of one material for another and changes in size are normally not patentable. Nor are ideas, suggestions, or business plans. Confused? Welcome to the wonderful world of dealing with patents.

A patent carries the right to exclude others from *making, using,* or *selling* an invention defined in the patent claims. A patent protects an invention and its functional equivalents. A simple design around may still infringe the patent if it performs essentially the same function in the same way to achieve the same result.

Patent Publications

You can write a letter to the Patent and Trademark Office, Washington, D.C. 20231, asking for a copy of the *Official Gazette,* the journal of the patent office. It lists and summarizes patents granted each week and some that are available for sale or license. The office also has other publications that might be of interest, including *Patents and Inventions: An Informal Aid for Inventors; Questions and Answers About Patents; General Information Concerning Patents; Patents and Government Developed Inventions;* and *Patent Profiles.* Copies of individual patents are available through the mail for $1 each. Also try your library.

The Small Business Administration also has several publications that might be useful, including *Ideas into Dollars;*

Avoiding Patent, Trademark and Copyright Problems; Introduction to Patents and New Product Ideas. Cost is $1 each from SBA, Post Office Box 30, Denver, Colorado 80201-0030.

Other Product Protection Methods

Patents are the only way to protect an idea—right? Wrong! In some cases patents are neither the best way to protect an idea nor even a viable possibility. For example, take Cabbage Patch dolls. Now, to my knowledge you can't get a patent on a strange-looking doll—even one with adoption papers.

But you can trademark the name "Cabbage Patch." A trademark is a brand name, including a word or symbol mark, which is consistently associated with a product to identify it and distinguish it from other products. Trademarks are acquired by actual use of the trademark in commerce. To gain additional legal rights you may register your trademark with the U.S. Patent and Trademark Office in Washington, D.C., and/or with similar state and trade organizations. You may also register an intent to use a given trademark with the U.S. Patent and Trademark Office. Trademarks last as long as they are used and therefore have a longevity advantage over patents.

You can also use copyrights to protect a product. In the case of the Cabbage Patch doll you could copyright each doll's appearance and the words that are used to describe it in packaging and promotional materials. A copyright protects original works of expression against being copied exactly. It does not protect the ideas that the works might express or variations of a styling theme. Such original works of expression that copyrights can protect may include: books, plays, poetry, labels, computer programs, recordings, advertisements, drawings, maps, movies, game boards and rules, photographs, catalogs, songs, sculptures, art reproductions, and most other original works of art. Since 1989 in the U.S. copyrights occur upon tangible creation of any covered original work of expression. You acquire additional rights by marking each copyrighted work with the word *Copyright* and © and the year of first publication, the name of the copyright holder, and the words *All Rights Reserved.* As an example, the copyright for a book might read "Copyright © 1995 Ronald M. Popeil, All Rights Reserved." Registering a copyright with the U.S. Patent and Trademark Office is necessary before you can sue for infringement, and registering within three months of publication allows you to recover legal fees in the event of an infringement suit. If you wish to register a copyright, call the U.S. Patent and Trademark Office in Washington, D.C., for details, or purchase a book on the subject such as *The Copyright Handbook* by Steven Fishman and published by Nolo Press. Libraries also often have trademark and copyright information.

Copyrights have a lifetime equal to seventy-five years for works made-for-hire or, for works not made-for-hire, an effective lifetime of the life of the creator plus fifty years. This again exceeds the life of patents.

Another method of product protection is to keep things secret. In the case of Cabbage Patch, you could keep processes used in the dolls' manufacture a secret. Such secrets, referred to in the law as trade secrets, are good for several reasons. First, they have an unlimited lifetime provided they are properly protected and secrecy maintained. Second, unlike patents, they protect your product instantly. The formula for Coca-Cola is a good example of a trade secret that has protected a major product for many years.

The problem with trade secrets is that they must be constantly protected. Employees having contact with the secrets must have specific agreements to keep such material confidential. Documents containing trade secrets must be marked

"Confidential." Confidential materials must be kept under lock and key. Once a secret is lost, it may be impossible to get it back, even if it is stolen. You may sue the thief for damages, but secrecy may be lost forever.

Still another way to protect products is to police the market for unfair competitors. In the case of Cabbage Patch, if someone came out with "Lettus Patch" dolls, the public might be confused as to whether the Coleco Toy Company, the creators of Cabbage Patch dolls, or someone else produced the new product. Under such circumstances you might be able to collect damages by suing the creators of Lettus Patch.

So what is the best method to protect your idea? In most cases you don't have to decide early in the game. As an example, you can apply for a patent, write "Copyright" on the product and associated promotional and packaging copy, keep aspects of the product a secret, and police the market for marketers who confuse the public—all without conflict. Even if you are trying to patent an aspect of your product that is a secret, there is no problem. Patent applications are held in absolute confidence by the U.S. Patent and Trademark Office (but not all foreign patent offices), and even if the patent office allows your patent claims, you can refuse to have the patent issued and thus preserve secrecy.

Insurance and the Underwriters Laboratories

If you are developing a product you should seriously consider insurance. Adequate insurance is a must, especially product liability insurance. Whether you're selling a product on television, in a store, or in a catalog, you'll need to provide "hold harmless" insurance. Depending on the product you select or the gizmo that you invent, you need liability insurance. If you have a knife, people can cut themselves with that knife. If you have a cosmetic, someone could get a bad reaction from it. This is why you need protection. Most retail stores require it.

If you're going to sell your product to retail stores, and your product is powered by electricity, it needs to be approved by the Underwriters Laboratories. Retailers won't even consider your product unless they see "UL Listed," on the package. (In Canada it's "CSA," and "VDE" or "TUV" or similar mark for Europe.)

You'll save some money with the UL approval. Your insurance will be significantly higher if you don't go through the costly UL tests. They can cost as little as $3,000 or as much as $20,000 or more, depending on how complex your product is and how closely it meets their specifications. UL's mandate is to test for public safety. Generally this means they test for fire, electrical, and mechanical hazards under the product's normal and abnormal operating conditions. If you don't pass the first time, you can, just as with a smog test, fix the ailment, and keep coming back until your product finally passes the inspection. However, you save yourself a lot of pain, grief, and money if you carefully read through their written specifications for your product category and follow them exactly.

Lawsuits

Soon after the infomercial for the Popeil Automatic Pasta Maker went on television, I received a threatening letter: a pending lawsuit if I didn't stop manufacturing my machine because of an alleged patent infringement. The letter was from Creative Technologies Corporation (CTC), a publicly traded company whose major product is a fourteen-year-old antiquated pasta machine. Was I violating their patent? I certainly didn't believe so. Before I came out with my product,

💡 MY THREE DISAPPOINTMENTS

The Inside the Outside Window Washer

"Washes the outside the same time you wash the inside"

PROBLEM: *Dirty windows in apartment buildings are hard to reach.*

Of the hundred or so products that I have marketed since the late fifties, I would consider all of them successes except for three. I always recall the Inside the Outside Window Washer whenever people ask me about my disappointments, but the truth is, I made money on it. Just not as much as I envisioned. I really expected a lot more.

•

I came across the window washer during one of my trips to Europe. I found this product over there that cleaned outside windows via magnets, but it was very expensive and needed additional development. Still, I loved the concept. If you live in a two-story house, or a highrise building, you know how often your windows are washed—hardly ever. Your windows are dirty most of the time. I lived in a highrise building in Chicago back then, and my windows were usually filthy. I figured there would be a lot of people like me who would want to live with cleaner windows. I was sort of right. But not quite.

•

I worked on a way to develop a product like this, but at a much lower price.

●

The product we came up with was made up of two handled units with a magnet inside each of them. A special wash-and-dry paper could be attached to it. On the outside of the window you placed one of the handled units. On the inside you matched up the other handled unit. As you cleaned the inside, you'd be washing the outside as well.

●

A cute story about our development phase: When we got our first production samples, we decided to test it on our office window. I started cleaning the windows and I moved the inside washer so fast that it disengaged from the outside washer, causing the outside unit to plunge sixteen stories down to Michigan Avenue, Chicago's premier shopping street, which was full of pedestrians. We raced to the elevator in a panic, afraid we might have killed someone.

●

There was a commotion on the street. The magnet had missed someone by a foot and a half, and he was the father-in-law of one of our executives.

●

I solved the problem by attaching a string to both pieces. That way, if it ever disengaged again for any reason, we could retrieve it, and it wouldn't bop someone on the head.

●

Anyway, we made the commercial, which I thought was very well done, and placed the product in our retail strongholds—stores like Walgreen's, Sav-On, or Woolworth's. The product didn't move as fast as we all would have liked. They were steady, but it wasn't like Christmas, when people bought my products in large quantities. Only the people whose windows were filthy and wanted them cleaned *today* came down. So a few weeks later the stores pulled the product, because the quantity being sold was not up to par with other TV products they stocked.

•

Ironically, the commercials did work; just not instantly. A few months later, when their windows were dirty, people came to the stores looking for the product, but it wasn't there. What it said to me was that people perceive their windows dirty within their own time frame.

•

So for me, the Inside the Outside Window Washer was a flop, because a flop is when you don't make the kind of money you anticipate. But it wasn't a loser. It didn't make big dollars, but it did make some money, just not enough to keep it on store shelves.

•

Today, the improved magnetic window washer is a big product over in Europe, but it's made by someone else.

The Hold-Up

"This is a holdup. Don't be held up. Get a Hold-Up."

PROBLEM:　*Where to put those phone messages and reminders?*

The Hold-Up was a fold-up. Another semiflop for Ronco. I was simply ahead of my time, from the wrong angle. Hold-Up was an adhesive sponge board that you could use as a bulletin board and attach messages, pictures, souvenirs, keys, and so on, to it. It was the flip side of stick 'em notes.

•

It was a clever idea, but unfortunately, people preferred sticking notes anywhere they wanted to. Another problem: Hold-Up was too conventional. There was no action. All it did was basically one thing—it held messages or little objects like pens, pencils, nails, tacks, et cetera. Next.

The Prescolator

"Brews your favorite fresh coffee instantly."

PROBLEM: *Getting a good cup of rich brewed instant coffee.*

Another product that was way ahead of its time. Today, in housewares departments and upscale coffeehouses, you'll find Melior type coffeemakers, which make quick, rich-tasting brewed coffee instantly. Well, that's exactly what the Prescolator did. But back in the early 1970s nobody cared.

•

I found the idea for the Prescolator during a trip to France, where similar products were quite popular. But my timing in bringing out an American version was all wrong. The Mr. Coffee type coffeemaker units were peaking in popularity at the time, and the public wasn't interested at the time in instant brewed coffee. If people are doing something every day, it's very, very difficult to get them to change their habits. If there are no serious problems with the old-fashioned way of doing things, they'll continue with their method, and that's a hard thing to break. There has to be a significant problem, otherwise it's an uphill battle. Making coffee was simple then, as it is today.

•

The difference is that coffee chains like Starbuck's have helped popularize the concept of richer tasting, good, flavorful coffee—in many different flavors. Many consumers want to take the Starbuck's type gourmet coffee tastes home with them, with products like the Prescolator.

•

The Melior coffeemakers solve the consumer's problem—poor-tasting instant coffee—by letting them drink their favorite blends of fresh coffee instantly. The Melior type products are out there, but they're still not selling very well.

•

And that's it for the disappointments.

I went to two major law firms to seek their opinions and sought as well the advice of my associate Alan Backus, who, in my opinion, is as good as any patent lawyer. All three agreed that I wasn't infringing anyone's patents.

I responded to CTC's letter by asking the court system in California to verify that I was not infringing on their patent. Then CTC countersued me for patent and copyright infringement and some other alleged transgressions, which were brought before the Federal Court in California, even though my machine didn't look or function like the pasta maker described in their patent. We won. We received a summary judgment from the court—something that's very rarely given in patent cases. A summary judgment is given when the acknowledged, uncontroverted facts indicate that as a matter of law one side is entitled to a judgment in its favor. So I won the case. The other side will probably appeal, but even if we go to trial, I'm confident we'll win. Still, it cost me $300,000 in legal fees before getting the welcomed summary judgment.

I point out this lawsuit to bring up the other side of knockoffs. If you're successful, people are going to sue you. So be prepared and get yourself a good lawyer now. Lawsuits are part of the business game today. If you have a successful product, you know you're going to be knocked off. You know you're going to sue or be sued. Someone else may deem you as the one who's doing the knocking off, even though your design is different and you really haven't violated any of his intellectual property rights.

Fighting off lawsuits is expensive and there's nothing you can do to prevent them. Let's just hope you're successful enough with your product and make lots of money, because if you're a hit, the vultures will start showing up at your door.

Key Points

1. Just applying for a patent can be as effective in fighting off competition as receiving a patent. It's much cheaper and can protect you within days.

•

2. Getting a patent is a costly and very time-consuming process. It can take as long as three years.

•

3. Visit the Washington, D.C., patent office (or hire your own patent search firm) to look up past and current patents. This will save you attorney fees for patent searches.

•

4. If your product is a hit, two things are almost inevitable—you will be knocked off with a clone of your product and someone will probably try to sue you for patent or copyright infringement.

CHAPTER 16

Design, Packaging, and Pricing

Now the fun begins.

After you have invented or found your product and tested it, you're ready for production. This is a very important step, because it defines what your profit will be. Everything hinges on what the product will cost you.

There are two primary costs: labor and material. Materials are usually slightly less overseas than they are here. From an overall standpoint plastic is pretty much the same price everywhere. Specialized things like motors can in fact be purchased for a lot less overseas than domestically. That's why you see most motors made overseas and imported.

A bagel cutter and a knife can't be made much cheaper overseas, and there is a marketing benefit to saying "Made in the USA." It helps our economy, and several large chains like to stock and advertise items that are made here. Wal-Mart takes pride in that.

It probably makes financial sense to have an electrical kitchen appliance made in the Orient. If you have a simple product, just something molded, it's not labor intensive, and you're not in the electronics area, then this country is fine.

The key in determining whether to have your product made overseas or here is this: If you can afford to do it here, you should do so. Some 90 percent of my products were made domestically.

I've always been a strong believer in "Made in the USA" because it's much easier to keep close tabs on the production. Having a product made overseas creates all sorts of problems that I'd rather not deal with. When I've strayed, it hasn't been solely for financial reasons. The Pasta Machine, for instance, is made in Asia because it's a highly technical product and they have a good track record with products of this type.

But let's face it. Nine times out of ten, products are made overseas because of the costs. When a product is very labor intensive, people go to areas of the world where the labor force does not get paid as much as here. It comes down to pure economics. The question you need to ask is: "Is it worth it?"

Yes, you will save money overseas, but you could also encounter problems with quality, language, timing, labor trouble, shipping strikes, political upheaval, and all sorts of other things. You have to examine both sides of the coin very carefully. *Only go to the Orient to produce products when, in fact, your product is labor intensive.*

Overall, products made in Japan are of high quality. My thoughts on other countries:

- Korea. *Quality.*
- Taiwan. *Be careful.*
- China. *Be very, very careful.*
- India. *Be very, very careful.*
- Mexico. *Be very, very careful.*

I've never had the opportunity to source product manufacturing in Europe, and so I can't really comment other than to observe that the exchange rate is currently not advantageous.

Now, if you do decide to make your widget here, where do you go to have it manufactured? In every city there are mold makers, professionals with injection molding machines, who can assist you in making your tools and dies or direct you to tool and die makers they know of. Look them up in the Yellow Pages, and begin this process by getting as many bids as possible.

Never just give the job to the first bidder. You'll be amazed at the range in bids you'll get when you go to several shops. It isn't just that several companies will try to underbid each other, it could be that one operates more efficiently than another or may have equipment capable of more economical production. Maybe one company specializes in your kind of product, while another doesn't.

The molder can take your prototype, weigh it, and tell you how much plastic is needed. You'll then know what your material costs are and get several bids to compare. Make your decision on whom to sign with not only on price but on track record. Who produces the best-quality product? Check on other companies these people have done business with. This process need not take a month—it could be done in a week. (Also, have your vendors sign a confidentiality agreement at the start of the job. No use having your business leaked to your competitors.)

Pricing

The million-dollar question: *How much will the consumer pay for my product?* You can't sell a coffee cup for $10,000.

You have to be realistic and have some idea of what's in the marketplace. And you obviously want to get as much as possible, to enable you to make a reasonable profit. What's the point of being in business unless you're going to make money?

I usually start by researching the competition. For my Food Dehydrator, for instance, I decided to price it at $129.95 because most of my competitors were at a much higher price. Years later, I dropped the price to around $60 in the Ronco infomercial. I had built a better mousetrap. I had no motor or fan, which allowed me to sell my product for a lot less (and allowed the machine to operate without making any noise). Also, I had no breakdowns because there were no moving parts. Thirdly, the energy costs were insignificant with my machine. And all I gave up was this: My Food Dehydrator took slightly longer to dry the foods than the motor-driven fan units. Instead of food taking a half a day to dry, it took a day. But folks were sleeping eight of those hours anyway.

In studying the prices of your competition, you need to know how their product is doing at whatever retail price it's being sold for. You do this by talking to salespeople who are selling it. I also want to know quantities, and this is where the trade magazines that I mentioned earlier can really help. They do a pretty good job of tracking sales. Every industry has a trade publication to track the hits, whether it's *Billboard* for the music Top 40, *Variety* for movies and television, or *HomeWorld* for housewares. Knowing this information can really help you come up with a realistic price for your product.

Don't limit your research to the selling points of your direct competitors—look into the entire category. If I had sold my Pasta Maker for $1,000, no one would have bought it. I choose four easy payments of $39.95, or $160, not only because it was less than my competitors (they were $175 and up) but because bread machines and other fancy electric kitchen items were selling for $200 and up and moving like crazy.

> **What should your cost of goods be in relation to your suggested retail price? No more than 25 percent. If your widget costs $20 to $25 to make, it should retail for around $100. That's my rule of thumb.**

Say an item costs $20 to make. Once you factor in overhead, packaging, amortization of tooling, and all other miscellany costs, your cost of goods is $28. The retail store will probably pay $60 for it, but how much did it cost you to sell it to the store? Did you go through a rep? If you did, the rep will make 8 percent of the wholesale price. So you really only get $55 of the $60, a gross profit of $27.

Now what will your advertising costs be? How much money from each sale will you dedicate to the cost of advertising? If you don't advertise, your product will just sit on the shelf and not move, because no one will know anything about it.

When we aired one- and two-minute commercials for a product, we tried for at least two TV exposures every day in the market. With infomercials one or two showings in a given TV market every week on a reasonably good station may be adequate.

I can't quote you an exact percentage or the amount of dollars to expend, because it will be different in each marketplace. Every product is different, and every TV station has a different price for airtime. But you should be prepared to spend money on advertising—it's doubtful you'll be successful if you don't advertise.

I can tell you that for my Pasta Machine, $60 to $100 of the $160 retail price is for media costs. (The exact amount varies from market to market.) Sometimes we don't make a lot on the initial sale, but there are so many other opportunities that come afterward: outbound marketing, the selling of customer names, and more marketing possibilities I will discuss later in this section. We couldn't do any of that if the customer didn't call in the first place and order the machine for $160, plus shipping and handling.

For most of my career I was a gadget guy. I sold items for $10 and $15, $9.99 and $7.77. Now I'm into more expensive items. It's much easier to deal with the high cost of media when you've got big profit margins. The only problem is that the higher the price, the fewer units you're going to sell. A lot more people can afford $20 than $100. But people tend to be satisfied more with the upscale items and also remember them more, which means more repeat business.

The money-back guarantee is avidly used by customers all over the country. There are a variety of reasons for returning goods. Some that come to mind are:

> —I spent more money than my budget would allow.
> —I loved it, but my husband said we didn't need it.
> —I purchased it because I was caught up in the sales pitch, but I changed my mind once I got it.
> —I was dissatisfied.
> —I ordered two of them, but I only need one.
> —It was bigger than I remembered it on TV.

And even though we have an extremely low percentage of product failures, we must include that in the list as well. The reasons are endless.

Naming Your Product

In getting your product to the consumer, a great name can really help make the sale. I don't believe in gimmicky titles, but prefer descriptive names that tell you exactly what the product is. The Popeil Automatic Pasta Maker. The Ronco Smokeless Ashtray. GLH—Great Looking Hair. Mr. Microphone. Very simple and easy to understand.

Back in the 1950s and 60s we used words like *miracle* and *amazing* a lot. Some TV stations gave us a hard time about *miracle,* in talking about the Miracle Brush, Miracle Broom, and Miracle Sander. They felt that some of the products were not miracles as we know miracles today. However, most of the stations did agree to let the ads on.

We believed the word *miracle* was a lot stronger than *amazing* or *new.* Of course the "*New Miracle*" or the "*New Amazing*" added even more impact, and then, one of our other favorites was *revolutionary* as in "*the New Revolutionary,*" or even better, "*the Revolutionary New Miracle.*" We did that on live demonstration a lot. It gave the consumer the perception of something above and beyond the normal product.

Were we stretching? Yes. But such hyperbole will continue to be used in mass advertising for hundreds of years to come, because it works. When you start bunching too many of them together—as in "*the Amazing New Miracle Revolutionary* (product)," that's overkill and insulting the intelligence of the consumer, and you don't want to do that.

New and Improved is not going away either. It's worked too well in the past. The same with *suggested retail price.* It's a fixture in the packaging hall of fame, because it gives the retailer a chance to show how the product is being discounted, and people always want a deal.

💡 THE TRIM-COMB

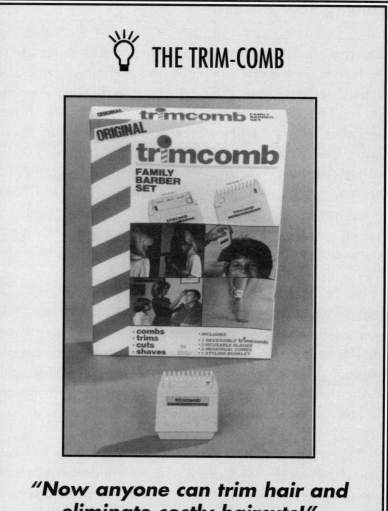

"Now anyone can trim hair and eliminate costly haircuts!"

PROBLEM: *The costs of haircuts when you have a lot of kids.*

Going to the barber to get a trim and forking over $5 or $10 isn't too bad if it's just you, but if you have four or five kids, you're talking

$25 or $30. My father's solution to the expense of haircuts was the Trim-Comb, a product that saved consumers many dollars.

•

The Trim-Comb—which we give away today with the GLH hair product—is simply a small plastic comb with a razor blade inside of it. It was a great little invention, a low-cost, high-margin item that made both of us lots of money.

•

And how good were the Trim-Comb haircuts? As good as the person doing the cutting.

•

"It trims, thins, shapes, blends, and tapers. All you do is comb. Get the Trim-Comb, styling booklets, a supply of blades, and a sturdy case all for $2.99. Practically the cost of one haircut."

•

Okay, it didn't slice or dice, but you could say this of the Trim-Comb—

•

"It trims! It thins!"

The Gift Box

You can get away with shipping products via mail order in plain boxes, but since sooner or later you'll want to be at retail, where the really big money is today, you're going to need clever, marketable packaging. Store buyers will demand it of you.

Don't underestimate the costs of the retail packaging. For my Pasta Machine it's $1.67 per box! Still, it adds information and helps my product presentation.

For products like some cosmetics the product is minor and the packaging is major. What beautiful bottle can I put this powder or cream into? Use your package to sell the same points you would use in a TV commercial: Why the customer wants your product. How it solves a problem for them.

Because shelf space in stores is so hard to come by, the retailer can get more small packages in his department than large packages, so you have to weigh those concerns before you put out your package. If it's too small, it doesn't have a high perceived value to a lot of customers. If it's too big, they may not want to carry it. A lot to think about. Decisions, decisions, decisions.

My packages are loaded with information on them. I point out the benefits of my products and give the consumer as much information as I can to help him or her decide to buy the product. I don't sell just one or two key points but instead usually list the advantages of my product and all of its uses. You can read my boxes across the room. That's important. You know what's in the package and you know what it does just by looking at it.

Besides the "As Seen on TV" logo, which is standard, I've also recently started putting my picture on the boxes. This helps sales because people see me on TV and then they see my picture on the boxes. They remember the demonstrations I've done and it helps differentiate my product from others.

As Seen on TV

I wasn't the first guy to use those magic four words on my packages and I certainly won't be the last. These words really do mean a lot. It's pure association to consumers who walk into a store. This is the product they saw on TV. Not the other one on the shelf, but the one they're holding in their hands.

They know how it works, because they saw the guy on TV demonstrating it. Maybe they didn't buy it then, but this is the one they heard about. Many of my competitors use the phrase *As Seen on TV* when, realistically, it never was.

Say you're walking through a store, looking for a gift for someone. You spot the product that you saw on television a month ago, and thought, *Gee, I wanted to get that product, but I didn't write the 800 number down and I didn't know how to order it.* And there the product is.

The one you saw on TV. And a sale is made.

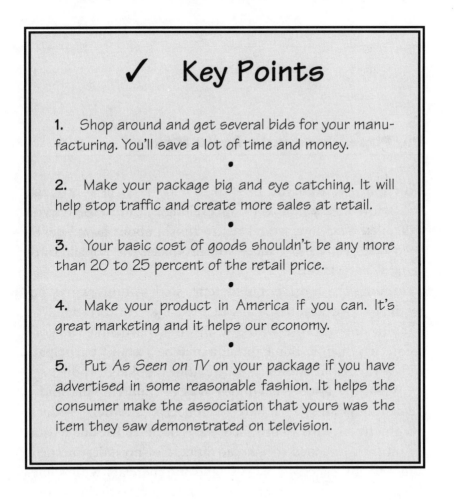

✓ Key Points

1. Shop around and get several bids for your manufacturing. You'll save a lot of time and money.

•

2. Make your package big and eye catching. It will help stop traffic and create more sales at retail.

•

3. Your basic cost of goods shouldn't be any more than 20 to 25 percent of the retail price.

•

4. Make your product in America if you can. It's great marketing and it helps our economy.

•

5. Put *As Seen on TV* on your package if you have advertised in some reasonable fashion. It helps the consumer make the association that yours was the item they saw demonstrated on television.

CHAPTER **17**

From Idea to Reality

The Popeil Automatic Pasta Maker

Now that I've told you how to develop your new product, and before I tell you how to start selling it, I want to give you a detailed overview, from start to finish, about how I developed one of my most successful products, the Popeil Automatic Pasta Maker.

Among the most popular items sold in housewares departments are automatic bread machines. Unfortunately, I was not one of those who got into that particular category before it got hot. But I thought maybe I could participate with a variation: another upscale home cooking product.

When my Food Dehydrator was off and running and a tremendous success, I had to conceive another product. Eventually, as with all products, sales declined for one reason or another. I needed to take advantage of my sales momentum and my success on QVC and infomercials with something new. So my thoughts went to how successful bread machines were. Bread machines had been popular for six years. So why not innovate a better mousetrap—a pasta machine?

Well, people eat pasta like they do bread. And they're willing to go out and buy an automatic bread maker and make it themselves rather than just go to the store and buy a loaf. Why? Because they can say they did it themselves and there are no additives and preservatives. They know what ingredients went into it, and there's nothing like smelling fresh bread in the morning. Could I make a pasta machine that was so simple that anyone could use it? That was my goal.

There were a few pasta competitors in the marketplace, but most of them didn't work very well. Most units required you to make the pasta by hand. That was tedious and a lot of hard work to get the result. Additionally, the people making pasta machines did a poor job of marketing their product, so sales were not great.

So competition was minimal. That's good news for developing a product.

Then I looked at what I didn't like about the existing pasta machines. Besides the fact that they didn't work very well, I also felt they were too big, bulky, noisy, and heavy. So I set out to build the best pasta machine that had ever been made, *and it had to be automatic.* No fuss, no mess. You don't have to be the first person to make a pasta machine to invent one. You're an inventor if you create a better pasta machine.

Not everybody has a big kitchen. A lot of people live in apartments. You have to keep that in mind when creating a housewares product. I set out to make a pasta machine that was quiet, small, very simple, and easy to use.

I went to my designer, Alan Backus, and told him what I wanted to achieve. I usually begin by telling him the shape I have in mind. I can't draw a straight line, so I describe what I'm looking for to Alan, and he draws several diagram possibilities. I know what looks good and I'm adept at putting my feet in the shoes of the consumer. I knew I wanted a clear container on top so the consumer could see the pasta being made and I wanted the unit to be relatively small because of lack of storage space in many kitchens today.

Alan presented me with six or seven different possibilities. The routine is that I'll choose one, and then Alan will take the design and convert it into something that's functional. For instance, if you look at the basket of the clear area of the Pasta Maker, you'll see ridges on the inside. That kind of breaks up the dough on the inside as it swings around. It's functional, yet it doesn't affect the outside appearance.

A month later, after much discussion ("How many dies do you want, Ron?") Alan came back to me with a finished design. I wanted more dies than anyone else was giving with their machine. If the industry standard was eight, I wanted twelve. I chose a round design versus square. And I wanted the *Popeil's Automatic Pasta Maker* product name in a very visible area.

Prototypes and Problems

Now Alan brings me a prototype with a rough design, and we start examining the problems. Our motor is reversible. It goes forward and backward. Wait a second. Isn't that like taking a car and throwing it into forward motion and then throwing it into full reverse? Won't that hurt the motor? Answer: I believe so. It will take its toll on the motor and the motor won't last very long. How long will it last? No one seems to know.

So we hire people to test the motors, all day, working with the machines until they stop running. That's why, when you switch the unit from Mix to Extrude, before it kicks in, there's a pause. It allows the motor to settle down before going into reverse or forward positions.

Now we're four months ahead. At this point most companies would have taken a year, between all the committees and different people who would have to sign off on each portion of the development. But I'm focused and I have talented people and I make all the decisions, so things move much quicker. There's no corporate infighting between one person who wants to do it one way and another who wants it another way, because I have the final say. It may be autocratic, but it works.

Now, we really want to put the prototype through the wringer, because there's a lot of complexity to pasta machines. We know that a lot of big companies have tried to make them work and failed. So I'm taking a shot at something they weren't able to do successfully. But I have an edge. I have the marketing and manufacturing know-how. If anybody can make a success out of this product, I can.

In the research we did, I wanted to pinpoint the major fault of the other pasta machines. What made consumers return them? We discovered that dry flour going through a die by itself will cake up and cause the machine to break down. Obviously, that was a problem we wanted to deal with. I didn't want to see 25 percent of my machines returned.

We worked on it and came up with a solution. If we put a little hole in the chamber, the flour could escape from it and not go through the die but instead go through the hole. And it was a patentable idea.

Motor Noise

So now we have the prototype and we discover that there is just too much noise from the motor. How do we get a quieter motor? It turns out that the noise isn't the motor, but the gears. They're meshing together. Okay, then, try different gears. So Alan and his team go off and experiment with different gear designs.

They come back a few weeks later with quieter gears. Now we have to find someone to build the motor for us, someone who has produced motors for quality kitchen appliances that have a lot of stress on them. So we search the marketplace for products that chop and grind electrically. Who makes these motors? How long have they been in business? Are they known for quality motors?

We find our motor, and it's made in China. The firm has a history of producing quality motors for these kinds of products—blenders, graters, and food grinders. I ask detailed questions of Alan about the firm: "*Who have these people done business with before? Show me what they've made before.*" Turns out they've worked with million-dollar companies. That's who I want to do business with.

So now we have the motor problem solved.

Pasta Scissors

I watch the pasta coming out of the prototype and say, "I want to cut the pasta off. Can't we put something on the outer edge of the product that will cut the pasta?" It doesn't have to be mechanical or motor driven, just something that consumers can move with their hands to swing it around. Alan says it could be positioned on the side, and we now have pasta scissors. That's one of the "goodies" of the machine that we put in for our design patent.

Production

Now it's time to figure out where to have the machine manufactured. Getting enough product is something to be concerned about. Are you going to give it to someone who's capable of producing large quantities? You want to make sure it's not being done in someone's garage. These people had to be searched out.

We chose a plant in Korea, because they had a relationship with the company in China that was making the motor. This company did a lot of work for Motorola on their appliances. We went to inspect their factory and it was very clean. In Korea you never know what to expect. It's either the very best or the very worst. There's no middle of the road.

We could have made the Pasta Machine here in the U.S., but the price would have been 30 to 40 percent higher. If I'm going to get the same quality in both places, naturally I'm going to take the less expensive one. Additionally, I have a very complicated product and the Asian factories are more adept at electrical devices.

Tooling

After you design the product you have to make the tooling, the steel molds you use in the factories to actually make the product. You can buy the motor outside, but it has to go into something.

So after the design is finished and you've approved the materials, the next thing you need to do is have tooling drawings made. We don't do that in-house, we hire a company to do that. After the drawings are finished, we take them to a tool and die maker. He cuts the steel that makes

💡 THE RONCO BOTTLE AND JAR CUTTER

"An exciting new way to recycle throwaway bottles and jars into decorative glassware, centerpieces, thousands of things."

PROBLEM: *Why throw away pretty bottles and jars?*

The creation of this product began with a simple question: What do people do with wine bottles after the wine has been drunk? Why throw the bottles away? Why not instead turn them into beautiful glassware?

•

Because of my early financial success I was always attempting to search out great bottles of wine. My favorite was La Romanée Conti, circa 1959, which was rated as one of the finest Burgundies ever. I have been told that only 325 cases of the wine were made that year. So now that you have one of the rarest bottles in your possession, isn't there something you could do with the bottle afterward, instead of just tossing it in the garbage?

•

At the time that I posed this question to myself, I happened to be in a hobby shop where I came across a product that used a glass cutter to take wine bottles and make them into beautiful glassware. Now you had a beautiful, heavy glass, but the edges were very sharp. Still, by using some emery paper, you could sand down the edges that would come in contact with your mouth, make it smooth, and *voilà*, you had a beautiful drinking glass, along with a label that said "La Romanée Conti 1959." Here was something you could look back at for many, many years; something that would probably end up being an antique.

•

The product I saw had been patented, and it did not work on odd-shaped bottles, such as a mason jar shape or a triangular-shaped bottle. It only worked on round, wine type bottles.

•

So I went to Connecticut-based designer Herman Brickman to see if he couldn't help me. "Herman," I said, "we have to create a product that not only works on wine bottles but all-shaped bottles, so the consumer can create not just wine-bottle mementos but planters or ornamental decorative glassware as well."

> •
>
> The process of developing the product took over a year, but we finally did it, and when it came out, it was a big success. It helped develop a new niche for Ronco: the "hobby" market.
>
> •
>
> *"A hobby for Dad, craft for the kids, a great gift for Mom. The Ronco Bottle and Jar Cutter. Only $7.77."*

the molds. Then the molds are sent to another company, a plastic molding firm. Tool and die makers and plastic mold makers are listed in the Yellow Pages. These shops can help you find out about and often refer you to people to make drawings as well.

When the parts start coming out and the motors are delivered, the manufacturer has to get the assembly lines functioning properly and efficiently. That doesn't happen overnight. It could take a month before they're smooth.

Initial Orders

How many should we make at first? You start with a small quantity to develop your sales pitch and also to test the product itself. Does it work? How long will it last? Does the consumer like it? A small quantity will cost you more per piece than a large quantity. If the consumer likes the product and your sales presentation has been perfected, you can then start talking about greater quantities to get better prices and begin your full-scale marketing campaign. But always start relatively small.

In my case, our initial order was based on how many my Korean manufacturer could produce. At that time it was 6,000 pieces a week. I wanted to have at least a couple months' supply before I went on television. I didn't want to be out there without at least 30,000 machines. This is something I would do because I have the experience. For the novice it's better to produce a small quantity and start off slow. You can buy 30,000 pieces after you get the experience. If inventing and marketing are new to you, you can't be a shooter. If you already have the experience, and the financial wherewithal, to do it, you should go for it, because there's also a downside to being slow.

Starting slow allows your competition to come in quickly. It's a judgment call. But if the retail stores have your product *before* your competition, your competitor would have to think twice before coming to the marketplace. If you use the formula of 20 percent of your retail price as cost of goods, it shouldn't be difficult to unload your product, in a worst-case scenario, slightly above your cost because it would be well below the existing market price for similar type products.

Tweaking the Units

Now the machines are coming off the assembly line, and we have to work with the manufacturer on putting them together.

I changed the assembly line around many times over there to fine-tune it. We had to swap materials. Before we sold the first unit, we found, through our extensive testing, that some parts weren't holding up as well as we'd thought they would. So we replaced them. You have to tweak your machine before the first piece is sold. That's how you end up with a quality product.

Now it's ready to be sold, and I truly believe ours is by far the best automatic pasta machine ever made. Why does ours work when the others don't? First, we had the benefit of analyzing and testing the older machines from our competitors. More important, we had talent and a better design.

Patents

Once we've applied for our patents domestically and the machines are working properly as they are coming off the assembly line and we know we have a success, we have one year to tie down our patents worldwide. We are protected by law for one year worldwide after applying for our patents domestically.

We don't apply for a patent of a pasta machine. You can't. You can patent different aspects of a pasta machine. Like the way my pasta scissors work. I don't know if I'm going to get it, but I've applied for it. Most likely I will be successful. There are other unique areas that make the machine function the way it does, and we've applied for patents in those areas. The fact that I've applied for patents keeps competitors from making knockoffs or direct clones of my product. That's the goal, anyway.

"If you invent a product," wrote Leslie Brokaw in *Inc. Magazine,* "you'll have one main goal when you come to the marketplace: getting people to be receptive to your unique offering. But if popular acclaim comes your way, it can be as much a liability as an asset. Competitors either imitate or one-up successful ideas, and defending your market against encroaching opponents is a different and complicated challenge.

"It's easier for rivals. They simply respond to your winning strategy with alternatives. You're expensive? They're cheaper. You offer a dozen choices? They've got one—styled after your best-selling selection."

Business is not easy.

Pricing and TV

In my research on other pasta machines, I found machines selling for anywhere from $175 to $250. I wanted to sell mine for less, offer a better machine, and more interchangeable dies (shapes of pasta) than anyone else out there. I chose the $160 price point because my competition was selling for more, and because I had tested two different prices on TV—$140 and $160. I sold as many at the $160 price as I did at the $140 price. I didn't need to be a brain surgeon to know which price to go for; however, I realized that if I sold my product for a straight $160, I would lose a lot of customers who wanted to purchase the product but didn't have the ready cash or could not deal with that expenditure on their credit card. So I created the four easy payments of $39.95, stealing a page from the Fingerhut catalog book, and that proved to be very successful.

I then had to figure a way to convert those four-pay customers to one-pay (better to be paid in full than to bank on the future). I accomplished this by offering the four-pay customer my Ronco Electric Food Dehydrator at a major discount over the phone. A high percentage of the people who called, expecting to make four payments, converted to a one-pay when they heard about my offer, which allowed me to make an additional profit from the dehydrator. That's effective marketing.

(Of course they could still pay the credit card company and/or make payments.)

My marketing plan is simple. A less expensive, better, easier product, available in four easy payments of $39.95. I

THE RONCO RHINESTONE AND STUD SETTER

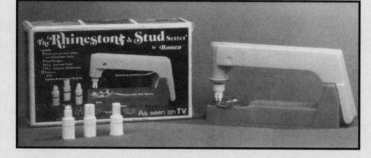

"It changes everyday clothing into exciting fashions!"

The Rhinestone and Stud Setter was our sequel to the Bottle and Jar Cutter, and again was developed by Connecticut-based designer Herman Brickman. The product was very simple: It put rhinestones and studs on jackets and jeans.

•

"Mom will love her Rhinestone and Stud Setter, not only for clothes," we said on the commercial, *"but for creating decorative handbags, hats, and patterns on pillows. For young and old. It's great fun!"*

•

One big mistake: I could have owned the tooling, but I didn't want the expense of it. I wasn't very smart, because I was paying for the tooling indirectly via my initial order purchase, which ran in the tens of thousands. A manufacturer would be foolish not to amortize the cost of his tooling into the finished product he is selling. I'm sure that if I

THE SALESMAN OF THE CENTURY

had asked Herman for the ownership of the tooling, he would have given it to me because my initial order was so large.

•

True, I made some good money on the product, but Herman eventually made much more, because I didn't ask him to throw in the tooling. And some twenty years after we marketed the Rhinestone and Stud Setter, and I was back on television with the Food Dehydrator infomercial, Herman took my old product, changed its name to the "Bedazzler," worked with another individual to sell it via infomercials, and made tons of money.

•

He didn't change a thing about the product except its name, and the infomercial was basically a takeoff on my old commercial that I made back in the seventies. I sure made it easy for him.

•

"For young or old, the Ronco Rhinestone and Stud Setter (or the Bedazzler) is great fun!"

made a new infomercial, bought media time, and the Pasta Machine really took off. I believe it will eventually be my biggest seller to date. As I write this in the summer of 1994, I've moved around $40 million worth of machines and have received more complimentary mail about the machine from my customers than anything else I've ever invented or marketed.

CHAPTER **18**

Ready for the Fair?

Okay, your product has been tested, the patent is pending, and you're ready to begin a TV marketing campaign. Logic says that going straight to infomercials or a home shopping channel would be the easiest place to begin—why bother with fighting to get in to see a retailer? Why not just wait for the phone to ring from the TV sales and bypass the middleman?

Because nine times out of ten you won't get in to see QVC unless you have a successful track record and they've seen a major successful TV ad campaign (either in infomercial or traditional short-form advertisement). And if you go straight to infomercial, you would probably lose money. (More on that later.) Finally, if you got in the door at QVC or HSN and got your product in their inventory, their customers wouldn't have heard of your item and your chances of selling would not be high. Their viewers respond better to preadvertised products, things they've already seen and heard about on television.

So where's the best place to start off, at minimal expense, to find out if you have a profitable product? Do as I did. Work the fair circuit. The fairs are even more popular today than they were back when I started some forty years ago. There's always hundreds of fairs in the summer and fall, tens of millions of people attend, and they come with money in their pockets.

Things have only gotten easier for the salesman since my early days. Credit cards are used commonly, so it's simpler to sell big-ticket items. Renting space at a ten-day fair can cost anywhere between $500 and $1,000. For a week or ten days you have the opportunity to take in a few thousand dollars a day, and you're only paying $50 to $100 a day for space. What a deal! Let's say the cost of your goods is 20 percent of the price you're selling it for (and it should be)—you can see how you can start to build proper equity.

To find out where the fairs are, look through a trade publication, such as *Amusement Business,* at the library. They print a schedule of all the fairs every year. (Check the Resource Guide on page 294 for *Amusement Business*—and other magazines' addresses.) Contact the manager of the fair, who will send you a form with the layout of the locations available. But before you send in your money and choose your location, find out how many people attended the fair or show last year. *Never purchase space for a fair that's opening for the first time.*

Start off by working a good local fair, and if that's successful, start spreading to other nearby fairs. Every state has a fair and most counties have a fair. There are also home, garden, and auto shows where you can rent a booth to sell products to the hundreds or thousands of people who come to visit on the weekend. Get ready to throw your product into the back of your car or truck, book a room at the Motel 6 or Super 8, and watch the money start to pour in. You could easily make $100,000 a year selling at these fairs and shows. The hours are long, but the profit dollars are high. You're your own boss. You're an entrepreneur.

Fairs are one of the best arenas in which to test-market new ideas and try out new prices. If the product doesn't move, lower the price. If it sells too well, then you know you're underselling. Better to find this out at a fair than in the midst of a big TV advertising campaign.

If your product is well received at these fairs and shows, you'll be able to hire other people whose main business is selling product at shows and fairs. They'll want to buy the product from you and sell it themselves at other fairs that you won't be able to attend. Many shows and fairs take place simultaneously.

If your product is demonstrable, then you're on your way to making your first commercial or infomercial. At the fair you'll develop your sales pitch, consumers will ask you every conceivable question in the world about your product, and you'll have the proper arena to polish your answers as well as benefit from testing your product over long periods of time, which is extremely valuable for product knowledge.

Once you start making money on the fair circuit, you'll probably want to do more and more fairs. Planning and organization for this are essential. The more fairs you attend annually, the more important scheduling becomes. Application deadlines must be met, booth fees or deposits paid, travel arrangements made. Like Willie Nelson or the Eagles, you're now on tour with your product!

You also want to put a little research into the subject, making sure you attend the right fairs. Why waste your time with an unproductive fair? How widely advertised is the fair, and what's the expected attendance? Overall I believe in sticking with state and county fairs, because they bring in the most people. But there are specific shows that might work for your business. Maybe your product would be good at an art or home-and-garden show. Maybe an auto show or health fair. These certainly bring in thousands of people as well. But where will the product booths be? In a good location, or far away from the foot traffic? Will the booths be inside, when the activities are outside? Will the weather be so hot at the time that nobody will want to go inside? Air-conditioning plays a big part, because if it's very hot, people will want to come inside to cool off. These are the types of questions you need to ask.

Once you're in, you've got to concentrate on one important thing—selling. Good sales techniques can mean the difference between success and failure at any fair or show. By good, I mean someone who gets out there and comes up with innovative ways to stop traffic and get customers to reach into their pockets. I'd hate to think that any of my readers would just sit in their booth and wait for potential buyers to stop and look at their product. That's certainly not how I did it.

I'm not saying you have to do what my brother Jerry did—he would lie down in front of the customers to stop them in their tracks. But you could subtly engage in a little hard sell. Smile at passersby, talk to them, tell them about your product. Encourage them to handle the product. Explain the problem that had existed and how your product offers a great solution. You have to keep in mind while doing this that you want to be talking to more than one person, so if I was stopping someone to shine his shoe, after the first shoe I would move to another, so that now I would have three or four people listening to me. Talking to one person creates only one sale. You're better off extending a little more effort and talking to eight or ten people at one time.

One of the most important elements for you at the fair—besides great salesmanship—is your booth. This is your storefront, your traffic stopper, your place of business. It

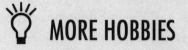

MORE HOBBIES

We had such great success with the Bottle and Jar Cutter and Rhinestone and Stud Setter, that we came up with many more hobby products. We had a home-making **Candle Kit,** a **Pottery Wheel,** which allowed kids at home to make small ceramics, and the **Ronco Flower Loom,** a home sweater/rug making kit.

•

They were all successful, but not huge hits. What they did was keep our name in front of the public as a company that was really good at coming up with new ideas, ones the whole family could enjoy.

•

Another fun hobby item was the Ronco **Ornamental Ice Maker.**

•

Anyone who's ever been to a wedding or party can picture the huge ice sculptures that are a major part of the party planning. Our product allowed you to make the same sort of sculptures on a much smaller scale—at home. We provided molds, which you would fill with water, and a few hours later, you had ice dolphins, lions, and other animals that made beautiful centerpieces. Ornamental Ice "makes your foods more appetizing and appealing."

•

"Great for parties, special luncheons and dinners, a must for birthdays, anniversaries, receptions, showers, any special occasion. Ornamental Ice adds elegance to any table and it's so easy."

doesn't have to be elaborate. In fact, you could buy one of those light portable booths that are advertised in the back of business magazines or simply rent an eight-foot table and put a nice cloth over it. Lining the back of the booth I always liked to stack up boxes of my product. That's the best advertisement you have. Plenty of product.

You'll also need electricity for lights, to focus in on the table, and a sign. You might want to consider having a sign made that you can hang on the back wall of the booth.

If you've got a great product and it's a hit, don't be surprised if someone else who is already in the infomercial business asks you to cohost their show. Don't do it. Do your own infomercial when the time is right. Their way, you'll make a little money, and it will seem like a lot at the time. But if you do it yourself, you'll make 160 times that amount. **Be in business for yourself!**

This is how I did it, and it obviously worked for me. Products like the Smart Mop, Ginsu knives, and even Birkenstock sandals began with sales at fairs. What most people don't know is that there are many people who still work the fair circuit today and make small fortunes. I know I could have easily become a millionaire staying at fairs. What I'm doing today isn't that different from what I did at the fairs, I'm just talking to a lot more people.

✓   Key Points

1.   Selling at a fair is a great way to test your product. It can also help establish your salesmanship and lead you down the road to infomercials and TV sales.

•

2.   Find a list of fairs and shows and start with a local event, then branch out to other fairs as you build your business and work toward getting on TV.

•

3.   Your booth doesn't need to be elaborate—just a demonstration table with a cloth around it, lots of product, and you.

•

4.   Before you put down money to exhibit at a fair, look at last year's attendance figures. Make sure the fair has a good track record of attracting crowds.

CHAPTER 19

Television, at Last

I've never been a billboard, radio, or newspaper guy. I've always preferred to get my message out through television, where the product is demonstrable. Some people have a way with words on paper and can sell that way. I opt for showing people my products and using the human voice to push the sale.

I believe that if I ran an ad in every leading newspaper in every city versus running a TV spot on the top TV station in every city, more people would see the print ad, but they might not stop and look at it. And if they did, would they stop and read the details? I don't think so.

That's why I like television. If you make an entertaining commercial or infomercial, people will stop flipping channels and listen to what you have to say. And for a guy like me who enjoys demonstrating his products, the infomercial is the greatest invention of all time. I finally have the time to tell my story the right way, where I don't have to cram everything into thirty seconds or a minute. I invite anybody to try introducing their product, tell all the problems it solves, show how it operates, tell the audience where they can get it, and announce the price—all in thirty seconds. It's not easy.

The infomercial business allows you to know how well you did yesterday today. And if you ship product out the next day, you'll have those funds in your bank account. In the old days of Ronco I used to have four people assigned to collections who did nothing but try to collect money for me from major retail outlets. The bigger they were, it seemed, the harder it was to get paid. They looked at your funds as a way of making interest, and the longer they kept it, the more money they could make. You could sue to get paid and be successful, but you'd end up hurting yourself in the long term, because the chains would never do business with you again. You couldn't win.

For as long as I can remember, people have been saying to me, "Ron, I have this idea for a product. It's a great invention, and I'd like to advertise it on TV, but I can't afford media." *They're wrong.* You can afford media. But it might be very limited media. You'd be surprised how inexpensive it is to advertise on local stations in the smaller markets outside the top twenty cities. (More on that later.)

800 Numbers

One of the greatest things that has occurred in my business is the advent of the toll-free 800 phone number. Thirty years ago most mail-order customers were not coming from New York, Chicago, and L.A. because these cities had retail stores that could handle their customers' needs. Mail order existed in those areas where they didn't have big, well-stocked stores.

It's different today, and for that I credit mail-order giants like Fingerhut, Hanover, QVC, and the Home Shopping Network. They made the 800 number a credible way to order product. Consumers today know that by ordering through an 800 number, if they don't like the product, all they have to do is send it back and they'll get their money returned. People used to think it was a hassle to return a product from mail order. No way. You put it on your credit card, and if you don't want the goods, it's taken off your bill.

Anyway, the 800 number opened up all these marketing opportunities in major cities for us and it's changed people's lives. People don't want to walk in six feet of snow in the winter to buy a product at a retail store. Instead they can just pick up the phone and have it delivered. It's so much easier to buy from an infomercial, cable shopping channel, or catalog. True, buyers can't feel the product with their own hands as they could in a store, but if you do a good job demonstrating it on TV, your customer will get a pretty good idea of your product's size, look, and how it works.

Telemarketing Companies

The first thing you'll need before you start your infomercial program is a good supply of toll-free 800 numbers, which are readily available from telemarketing companies.

What does a telemarketing company do? It supplies you with 800 numbers—hundreds if you want them. In my business I have over a hundred of them. That way you can track the sales of each TV station. Let's say, for instance, that I was running a campaign on three different stations in Las Vegas with 1-800-43-RONCO, 1-800-44-RONCO, and 1-800-45-RONCO. We could monitor the sales for the products based on each number and determine which station was giving us the best results.

The bigger the telemarketing firm, the more 800 numbers you'll have access to. I use a company called West Telemarketing, which is located in Omaha, Nebraska. When we say on TV, "*So call 1-800-43-RONCO—operators are standing by,*" these are the people we're talking about.

When you call, the operator will ask you which product you're interested in. You tell him, and he'll punch up all the pertinent information on the computer screen—the price, shipping and handling charges, and how long it will take to arrive at your home. He'll ask for your name, address, phone number, and credit card number.

Now, whether the customer buys or not, the telemarketing people still get paid, usually at a cost ranging from $1.50 to $5.00 a call. The longer the presentation, the more we have to pay. I write the scripts for the telemarketers to use to help sell the customer and to answer their questions correctly.

Upsells

We have all of our telemarketing firms engage in the fine art of "upselling" when customers call. When the customer's ready to order, we offer them a very special deal, for just a few more dollars.

The Pasta Machine, for instance, sells for $160 or four easy payments of $39.95, whatever the consumer selects.

If you put the Pasta Machine on TV and sold it for $160, it wouldn't be a mass item, because it's a big expenditure. Some people can afford it, but for others the price is too high. So we let them pay in installments. That presents a difficulty. It's not as severe with credit card customers because you can bill such people every month. But if they go over their limit any of those months, you have a problem—and they already have the product and are using it. We buffered that expense by adding the shipping and handling to the initial payment and as far as the bulk of the customers go who have chosen the four-payment plan, we do everything that we can possibly do to convert them to one-pay. The telemarketer who is taking the order will offer a free gift of some sort, an item that has a high perceived value, but doesn't cost too much to make. For instance, we're currently offering customers a large discount on the Food Dehydrator if they convert their four-payment plan to one whole payment. We're able to convert at least 20 percent of the people by offering this deal. You make money on interest and you're assured full payment on your product.

Once we have that handled, we move to upselling. Since we have the consumer on the phone, and she is in a receptive mood for buying the product, by offering an additional very special value that we hope she can't refuse, we'll add to her satisfaction and our profitability.

So when she's about to order, the operator tells her about our special offer: twelve different additional pasta shaping dies (types of pasta), which normally sell for $9 each by themselves, a four-way ravioli maker, and a video cookbook, all for just an additional $39.95, and no additional shipping and handling. "Can I add that to your order?"

Well, 50 percent of the people order the extra dies because they'd like to have them and wouldn't mind the ravioli maker and the cookbook video as well. So the $160 sale is now a $200 sale, and this represents another profit margin. Of the 200,000 Pasta Machines we've now sold on TV, some 51 percent were with the upsell, which, of course, meant greater profits.

Do I ever feel bad that the consumer calls expecting to spend $160 and walks away with a $200 bill on his credit card? On the contrary, I feel wonderful. The consumer got a great value. It wasn't like I sold him an empty box. *(Only undertakers sell empty boxes and get away with it.)*

We sell quality and value and we stand behind our product. So once we've created a sale, we want to enhance that sale and profitability by adding on something to the product, something so appealing that a major portion of consumers will take advantage of it.

And all of this costs money. It costs when people say,

"No, I just want the basic product." Because we paid for the telemarketer to explain all those things to the consumer. Remember, the longer the telemarketer is on the phone with the customer, the more we have to pay. That call could cost as much as $4 or $5. But if we receive an order worth $40 more, we've made money. And since 51 percent of our customers take the bigger package, our average sale is $180, more than offsetting the costs of the consumers who decline the extra die sets.

The Telemarketing Script

Here's what our telemarketing firm says to customers when they call 1-800-43-RONCO about the Pasta Maker:

"The Popeil Automatic Pasta Maker sells for $159.95 plus $17.90 shipping and handling, or four easy payments of $39.95. The shipping and handling is added to the first payment. California residents add sales tax.

"The Pasta Machine comes with twelve shaping dies, FREE recipe and instructional video, package of gourmet pasta flour, $100 in coupons for other products, and the $20 Popeil Bagel Cutter and Bagel Knife. There's a thirty-day money-back guarantee (less shipping and handling) and delivery is two to four weeks."

If they ask for the four easy payments of $39.95, we try to encourage them to pay for it all at one time, with an incentive.

"If we can bill you one time instead of four, then you can receive the $130 Ronco Electric Food Dehydrator for only $29.95. May we bill you one time instead of four?"

Then we do the upsell.

"We have a very special offer for you right now. You'll love our expanded accessory package. It includes twelve more additional different pasta shaping dies that make

shells, manicotti, and even corkscrew pasta. Now you can have all twenty-four dies the company makes. These shaping dies normally sell for $9 each. That's $108. In addition, you'll receive a four-way ravioli cutter plus a video recipe cookbook. This accessory package sells for over $150 and it can all be yours for only $39.95. And there's no additional shipping and handling.

"Would you like to take advantage of this special offer available only to first-time buyers? Believe me, it's really worth it."

I don't believe in leaving any stone unturned. Whether or not they agree to go for the upscale model, while we have them on the phone, we go for one more sale:

"If you'd like to buy a gift for a friend or relative, you can purchase right now one additional Pasta Maker, like the one you just ordered, for $50 off. Would you like to order one additional Pasta Machine? They make great gifts."

And then we go for the extended warranty.

"One more thing. The warranty on your Pasta Machine is for six months. Now you can take advantage of the company's new Extended Service Contract that follows your six-month warranty. It covers all parts and labor for additional years, for only $12 per year. For three years, that's only $36. Would you like to take advantage of this special offer?"

Lastly, if customers want more information, we refer them to the Ronco customer service phone number. And if the telemarketer isn't able to capture the sale, he or she presses one of eight buttons.

1. *Pricing or payment plan, caller requested.*
2. *Product information, caller requested.*
3. *Caller interrupted, will call back.*
4. *Misunderstood offer.*
5. *Refused to give order.*
6. *Did not want to hear upsell.*

7. *Caller disconnected. Prank call.*
8. *Other.*

Outbound Telemarketing

In telemarketing you have to anticipate that out of every hundred calls you get, 60 percent will be orders and 40 percent questions. That's bothersome, because as I said, we have to pay for every call, whether or not the customer buys. So we try to make back some of that lost revenue by capturing customers' names and phone numbers when they phone. We know there was some interest there, otherwise they never would have called.

We then turn their names over to an outbound telemarketing company. They pursue the caller later and make a second attempt to sell the product.

Is it an invasion of these people's privacy to do this? Not necessarily. I've already invested $3 or $4 in this person, because he or she called my toll-free line and spent some time with my telemarketing rep. You don't see the customer complaining about causing me an expense. It works both ways. Everything is on percentages. You will get a percentage of people who call and ask a variety of questions about the machine who don't order. And you will pay for that.

And those people who have called may just not be in the mood that day. Maybe they didn't like being spoken to by someone who was reading from a script. Maybe they'd appreciate more personal interaction with the experienced outbound telemarketer. Most times, that is the case, and we end up making the sale after all, although at a greatly reduced profit margin, because the outbound telemarketer gets a percentage of the transaction.

Credit Cards

If your customer is going to call your 800 number, you're going to need a relationship with a credit card company to collect your money. If it's checks and money orders, that's normally done by our fulfillment house. But that's just 10 percent of our business. Most mail order business today is via credit card. (On credit cards, in computing your cost per order, allow for at least 5 percent of your credit card customers not to clear. With checks it's a slightly higher amount.)

You've got to convince a bank that you're strong and healthy to take on as a credit card customer. Their greatest fear about people coming into this business is, if you're a start-up, what happens if the customer wants to return the goods six months later, and you're no longer there? Then the bank takes the heat.

Small start-up companies have to leave a bond with the bank or have to work with third parties who have access to that area of the business. These third parties will want a small percentage of the business that's transacted.

That said, you don't want to lose customers out there who don't have credit cards. These people do exist today. Some can't qualify, some just don't believe in them. They prefer to pay with a check, and so now you have to wait for the check to clear and you can't bank their money the next day. It's an inconvenience, but what's the alternative? **No sale.**

Product Delivered within Four to Six Weeks

You can't help but notice how most infomercials tell viewers that the product will be delivered in four to six weeks. Does it really take that long to get the product out of the factory, into a package, and to your home? Not necessarily.

TWENTY TOP HITS BY THE ORIGINAL STARS

PROBLEM: *The high costs of buying popular records.*

In 1970 K-Tel, a Canadian company that had promoted compilation records on television in the U.S., Canada, and Australia, began contacting our retail and television accounts and going after our business.

•

We felt turnabout was fair play—it was time for us to get into the music business.

•

My Ronco partner Mel Korey had a real talent for music—his childhood ambition was to be a successful songwriter. So getting into the music business finally for Mel was like a dream come true. When we successfully took on K-Tel and began to market compilation LPs, the success of the records was totally due to Mel. I had very little to do with the selection of music, or the making of the animated commercials that were used.

•

Compilation records were albums with usually eighteen or twenty hit songs by the original artists. You'd contract with the record companies and pay a set price and royalty based on the hit status of the song.

•

Back then, the songs would appear on the compilations many months after they had left the Top 40. Still, when we would release the albums, consumers received quite a value—twice the number of songs than they would on a regular album, at a price that was lower than hit records, around $3.99 or $4.99.

•

Our first compilation had an incredible all-star lineup, including the Beatles, Jefferson Airplane, Neil Diamond, Buffalo Springfield, the Turtles, and more. We put it together via a new antidrug foundation called Do It Now. They were able to convince the performers to donate songs, so that when we called the foundation, the album was basically already put together.

•

They licensed us the rights to the music, and we, in turn, promoted it on TV and marketed the album to retailers. The only provisos were that we had to call the LP *Do It Now* (which was fine) and put an antidrug message on the back of the record.

•

Now, we were against drugs, but remember, this was the early 1970s. We felt that if we put an antidrug message on, it would hurt our sales—teenagers were our target audience.

•

We got around it by putting the antidrug message in light pink on a yellow background. The only person who might be able to read it clearly would be Clark Kent. We sold over 500,000 albums, qualifying for gold status.

•

And now we were well on our way as record moguls, producing and promoting some four to six albums a year, all bearing the imprint: "*Twenty Top Hits by the Original Stars.*"

How fast the product is shipped depends on the availability of the product. We try to get it out as soon as possible, but it depends on what's in stock at that particular moment. We may be back-ordered on the Pasta Maker or the Food Dehydrator, so it may take an extra week or two to get them out to the consumer. Or they could be sitting in the warehouse and arrive at the customer's home in a week.

You have to be very careful about how you describe your shipping schedule or you could get into trouble with the Federal Trade Commission. (Like me.)

> **Important point: Whenever I speak to different organizations about marketing, I always make clear that if you're going to come into this business and sell products via the mail, be fully aware of the FTC and U.S. Postal Service regulations. They can be inconvenient and expensive, but they'll cost you a hell of a lot more if you run into a problem with those agencies—not only in dollars but in bad publicity and its effect on your reputation and sales.**

We once ran into a snag with the FTC because I didn't tell consumers in our infomercial when the product would arrive. I didn't want to say it would arrive within "four to six weeks," because I hoped we could do better. What I didn't know was that if you don't mention a time period, the FTC takes the position that it's thirty days, no ifs, ands, or buts.

This can present problems for you if the product is made overseas, or, as in the case of GLH, someone has ordered a hair color that is currently out of stock and awaiting production. Maybe it's a color that's not used very often and we're back-ordered. As much as you'd like for it not to happen, there can be time delays in manufacturing.

Our problem with the FTC arose because we were too successful. We received so many calls from customers, that they couldn't get through on the phones to our customer service reps with their questions. When I found out how severe the problem was, I hired more people to man the phones in our office.

But before we fixed the problem, when people called us and couldn't get through, they went to the FTC to complain. When the FTC investigated, they discovered that for some of the orders that hadn't been filled within thirty days, we had sent postcards to customers explaining the delay, promising to get the product out to them soon.

But that wasn't good enough. If you don't ship the product within thirty days, the rule is that you're supposed to send a postcard, tell the customer why it's late, when it will be shipped, and *offer to cancel the sale.*

We didn't do that. We did mail a postcard to the customers advising them that their product would be late; however, we didn't additionally offer them the right to cancel the sale. In fact the thought never occurred to us because we have a thirty-day money-back guarantee. The customers could have returned it after they got it. That didn't satisfy the FTC.

Initially, they thought our fine would be $40,000, but after their investigation they deemed it to be $50,000. How they came up with that number, when we didn't profit by even one dollar, I'll never know. "Ron," my friend Doug Briggs, a top exec at QVC, told me, "sometimes you get the turkeys and sometimes you get the feathers." I think in this instance I got the feathers.

Now our computer automatically kicks in if we haven't gotten the product out in thirty days, and we send a postcard explaining why—and we offer the consumer the chance to cancel the sale.

My good friend Joe Sugarman, who sells the BluBlocker

sunglasses on infomercials, ran into a problem with the FTC, and instead of settling with them like I did, he decided to spend a fortune fighting them. Personally, I'd rather have the money he wasted fighting the FTC.

Before You Get Started in Infomercials, Some Friendly Advice

With infomercials, the sales potential is enormous. You get twenty-eight minutes and thirty seconds to demonstrate your product and fully explain why it solves problems, and there's no middleman to get in the way of your message.

That said, the infomercial business is also very, very expensive. It costs anywhere from $100,000 on up today to make your program. Then you have to buy advertising time on TV stations, and infomercial time is very hard to get.

> **Going into the infomercial business today is a great way to lose money. Let me warn you that twenty-nine out of thirty people who go into infomercials *lose their shirts*. You don't hear about people losing money in infomercials; all you hear about are the successes. It's like a man going to the racetrack. When he loses money, he never tells you— only when he wins.**

Why are so many people failing? Because as infomercials have become more successful, stations have been jacking up the rates. If you pay too much for media you, too, will lose your shirt. So what do we do? We look for deals. The larger companies who have read about the infomercial revolution come in and gladly pay the going rate, not knowing that the prices were so much cheaper a month or even a week ago.

Buying TV time is your great unknown. It is all based on supply and demand. Every station in every market and every cable network, whether big or small, established or just starting out, will have a different formula on pricing. As the demand increases, the cost of the TV time escalates. For instance, I was running my infomercial for the Food Dehydrator on the CNBC cable network back in 1992. We aired Sundays at four P.M. Eastern Standard Time and paid $9,600 for the spot. Every time the commercial ran, we made $5,000 to $6,000 in profit, based on sales that came in for the unit.

And not only was the infomercial a hit for me, it was also very successful for CNBC. The A. C. Nielsen Co. did a report, which CNBC showed me, that said their audience doubled every time my infomercial aired. We have people in the industry trying to create shows that will get a big audience, and here's a twenty-eight-minute-and-thirty-second commercial pulling in a huge number of people to watch.

So what did CNBC do? How did they repay me for my ratings success? They raised the price of the spot from $9,600 to $20,500. They didn't increase their audience, they didn't buy another station, they didn't expand to more cities. I didn't even get a thank-you for doing so well for them. I got them more people to watch their network, yet my rates were being more than doubled. All because of supply and demand. Well, if I ran the ad at their new price I'd lose $5,000 every time the spot aired. I'm not in business to lose money, so I canceled.

Now, I knew what the ad used to cost and how many units I moved during that time period. But the new guy on the block who comes in and spends the $20,500—he doesn't know that it was half that price a week ago.

Who's paying the higher rates? Large companies, including *Fortune* 500 firms, who have heard so much about the infomercial business and how successful it can be, are prime candidates, and the buying agencies are encouraging them because the higher the price of their airtime, the more commission they make.

So you have concerns like Volvo, Apple Computer, Magnavox, General Motors, and Club Med calling their advertising agencies and saying, "Hey, let's take a small piece of our advertising budget and run some infomercials." But they don't flash an 800 number at the end to buy, so they have no way of knowing how many people they sold. The beauty of infomercials for me is that the next morning, I have a printout of how many people called in to buy. I have an accurate report on how effective my infomercial or short-form ad was. *I know today how much money I made yesterday.*

Well, no one's picking up the phone and saying, "Let me have a blue Volvo, the four-door with the radio, and put it on my credit card." The only thing Volvo knows at the end of the year is that it was profitable, and that they advertised on TV, and in newspapers and magazines. How will they know if the infomercial was the reason the consumer bought the car? They don't. But the TV stations will still continue to accept their money because the agencies that buy time on behalf of Volvo get top dollar for their services.

The more Volvo spends, the more commissions the agencies make. The client doesn't know what's really happening except that overall he's profitable or unprofitable for that quarter or the year. I don't know if he realizes that by his paying these exorbitant prices, people like you and me who invent, or who market products on television, are being priced out of the market.

Millions from Infomercials?

Most people think guys like me are making millions off infomercials, but it's just not so anymore. We did in the early days when it seemed like you could put anything on and people would buy it. Those golden days of infomercials are over. The TV exposure gets me into retail stores and onto QVC, where I make real money. On infomercials today, I do a little better than break even. But that's okay, because it gets exposure for my products. I preferred the early days of infomercials when I didn't need retail to make the real money, because retail stores can be a pain to do business with.

In July 1994, when I was writing this book, our profits on the Pasta Machine infomercial were $25,000 one week, $50,000 the next, back to $25,000, and then $75,000. Those figures include cost of goods and TV advertising time; they don't include overhead. Let's take the $75,000 week and say the overhead is half that amount. In a month that's $140,000 profit, well over $1 million for the year. To a lot of people that's a tremendous amount of money, but not to me, because in the heyday of infomercials we could make half a million dollars *in a week*. Making $30,000 in a week is no big deal after you've made half a million.

The Odds Are Against You, But . . .

So maybe your product is so unique and so spectacular that it could possibly handle being advertised in an infomercial. Maybe it's that one product out of thirty that will click. Be warned, however, that the chances of its doing so are very slim because everything has to be perfect.

- You must have the right product at the right price.
- It's got to be needed by lots of people.
- It's really got to solve a problem.

MIRACLE BROOM

"Cordless Electric"

PROBLEM: *Dirt.*

The Miracle Broom was an $11.99 portable vacuum that could pick up broken glass and nails, and get into hard-to-reach places. Was it a miracle product? No. It was very utilitarian, a very handy product to have. But it certainly wasn't a miracle.

•

If I brought the Rhinestone and Stud Setter or Miracle Broom back today, they'd carry the credibility of design and performance of what

I'm known for today. I'm sorry to say that in those days, I was limited because of the talent that worked with Herman Brickman, who also manufactured the Miracle Broom.

•

One of our expressions in selling the Miracle Broom was the term "cordless electric." People seemed to respond to those words, which was really just another marketing way to not say "battery operated—go out and buy some batteries."

•

I wasn't the marketing genius who created the term, but I certainly participated in spreading it around. We found in the 1970s and early 1980s that if you could get the word *electric* in there, in some way, sales would increase, because an electric product was always deemed to be superior. *Electric* was perceived as powerful and longer lasting. *Cordless electric* led the customer to believe the product was a lot more powerful than it really was. But with those words the consumer had to purchase two "D" batteries to make the product function.

•

"Great for car, boat, furniture, office, workshop, and hard-to-get places."

• You have to be able to move quickly on it, because someone out there is going to try and knock you off.

If your product meets all these criteria, but you find that you're a few million dollars short to begin your infomercial marketing, don't worry; there is a way for you to get there, it just won't happen overnight.

The key to the whole plan is sometimes taking things one step at a time. Be very methodical. Don't be in too much of a rush.

How to Buy Cheap TV Time

I don't know how many times in my life people have come up to me and said they wanted to get into TV marketing, but couldn't afford TV advertising. For some reason they always think national and never local. They've all heard that a thirty-second spot on the Super Bowl goes for $1 million or so, and that scares them away.

What they don't understand is that there are TV stations in small cities like Rockford, Illinois; Madison, Wisconsin; and Eugene, Oregon, all over the country where you can usually pick up cheap advertising time. You won't reach thousands of households, like you will in New York City, Chicago, or Los Angeles, but you will be able to get your message out to hundreds of people via local TV stations.

The easy way is to just buy a few spots on national cable. But that's expensive. The hard way, which is the right way, is to buy local and then maybe national time. It takes a lot more effort and a lot more work but it's worth it.

I started in this business by advertising on local TV, and that's where the bulk of my money is still spent today. Back when I began, we spent $200 a week advertising on local stations. In today's prices that would probably be $400. You can't tell me that a guy who wants to go into business can't afford to spend $400 a week to test his product.

Now understand that in this situation, I'm talking about the price of a one-minute or thirty-second commercial, the form that TV stations have the most inventory of and prefer to sell.

For infomercials the costs are much higher, but the concept is the same. You'll have a much easier time finding reasonably priced infomercial advertising time on stations in smaller markets than in, say, Chicago and New York.

The biggest problem you face in getting into infomercials is the price of TV airtime. It's all supply and demand, and stations have a lot more short-form one- and two-minute slots available to sell than they do for half-hour infomercial time.

And there are still some TV stations that won't sell half-hour blocks. They think it cheapens their image, or simply would prefer to air sitcoms or cartoons instead. But more stations are climbing on the bandwagon every day because of high profits. There are now more stations that sell half-hour time than those that don't.

The key to inventing products and marketing them on television is to make sure the product can deal with the high cost of media. Which isn't easy. It just takes a lot of careful planning to select time slots that are priced right.

Many major TV stations in the top ten cities sell infomercial time for between $8,000 and $45,000. Outside of the top ten, in smaller cities like Rockford and Eugene, you can buy infomercial time for as little as $900.

The most I ever spent, in fact, for infomercial time was $30,000, but that's very rare. I consider a $5,000 or $6,000 spot to be expensive. Ten percent of our weekly budget falls in the $5,000 to $25,000 range. The other 90 percent averages between $500 and $600 for half-hour infomercials in cities all across the country.

> **There are only so many slots open for infomercials (usually late night and weekend mornings and afternoons) so stations can price them however they choose. On a percentage basis infomercial time represents perhaps only 5 percent of the available inventory.**

Buy Slowly

The only way to make your first infomercial campaign work is to start off very slowly. As I've mentioned, we've put out close to $60 million advertising our Food Dehydrator on infomercials (and brought in over $100 million in sales), but that was over a three-year period.

Where did I get $60 million from? Cash flow over a long period of time. I started small, took my profits, and pyramided them, and the snowball just got bigger and bigger. It wasn't like I had $60 million sitting in a bank account when I started or after my first two weeks. My first expenditure was $40,000 a week. But because of the cash flow coming in, I slowly increased it, to the point where it eventually went as high as $500,000 a week per product. Media prices weren't that high then, so it was easier, but if I were just starting out today, I would take everything very slowly and pyramid my way up.

Produce a low-cost infomercial (our first infomercial for the Food Dehydrator cost just $33,000, but you'll have to spend more today; viewers expect glossier production values—you're looking at $75,000 minimum) and then test your spot in smaller markets.

- Buy two or three small cities and see how your product performs. I'm talking places like Sacramento, Las Vegas, Raleigh, or Bangor. You'll know in a couple of days whether you're achieving success or not. Just multiply the number of units sold by their cost and deduct this amount from the cost of TV time.
- If your TV costs were $1,000, and you sold a hundred widgets, whatever they may be, it cost you $10 each to sell them. If your cost of goods is $5 and you're collecting $35 from the customer, you know you have a winner.

- After you've tried your three or four stations and have achieved success, I recommend that you up the ante a bit and start spreading out. Whatever you do, don't rush out and up the ante to $125,000 on twelve stations after spending $12,500 a week on four stations for the first two weeks. No way. Maybe bump it up to five or six markets. *This is the safe play and the right play, to make sure you don't lose your shirt.*
- **Important tip:** I wouldn't buy time for the second week at all, because TV stations have a two-week cancellation policy. With the cancellation policies, if you found some dud markets, you'd be stuck with them if you purchased time for longer than seven days. But by purchasing TV time for just a week, you get your information, get rid of the buys that were not successful, and then look for additional time in other markets. The markets that were favorable in the first week, I'd buy around three weeks later.
- Remember the end goal: You want to start building toward more airtime where more people see your show. Do you want to get twelve orders and make a small profit or do you want to operate on four hundred orders and make ten or twenty times the profit? The bigger the audience, the more orders you'll capture, but the cost of your media will be higher. Also don't forget that it takes the same amount of effort to buy time on a TV station, whether that be Ottumwa, Iowa, or New York City. The same phone calls, the same conversations, the same analysis takes place.
- Once you're ready to spread out nationally, I would recommend spending no more than $25,000 tops for your first big week of TV selling. That's to get enough markets across the country to give you the information you need about major success or failure.

•

Spend a year building your pyramid very slowly, carefully going over your profit and losses, finding which stations provide the best results, at what time periods, with the goal of finally including Chicago, New York, and Los Angeles, the big three. A penny will become a nickel; a dime will become a quarter; a dollar will become ten dollars, and so on. When you start to make money, it grows. Your profits balloon as fast as you can buy time on other TV stations.

And when you're everywhere and the money is coming in faster than you can count it, you'd better start thinking about your next product. That's what I do.

Cable TV

Every day, it seems that another new cable channel is launched. In 1994, for instance, we saw new channels like fX, America's Talking, Turner Classic Movies, and ESPN2 come onto the scene. Wouldn't it be inexpensive and cost effective to make an advertising buy with one of the new channels for your infomercial? Yes and no.

Yes, it could be cheaper, but it might not be effective. Who's going to see your ad? These new channels don't have many viewers. You could take the information from your test, and if you're not successful, you might blame your product or ad, instead of the media. At least with Rockford, Illinois, you know the TV station has a loyal audience. When the station rep quotes you how many individual people they reach, you can believe him. I can't say the same about the new cable channels that claim to reach millions and millions of people when, in reality, it's the viewing audience that's important to you, not how many homes they are in—perhaps unwatched.

The bottom line is this: If you try and you're successful, it doesn't make any difference what the rep told you about the viewing audience. If he tells you there's a million people watching, and you didn't sell any product, what difference does it make whether he was accurate or not? Just please don't be misled by these fictitious numbers.

A new cable network like fX will charge you more than the Rockford TV station and you know Rockford has an audience. There are too many fX's out there, too many new stations launched; the more channels that come on line, the more you have a splintered audience. For us, advertising on most of the cable networks doesn't work because they're overpriced, even though they generate greater revenue than the small local TV stations. Of our total advertising budget, 98 percent of it goes to local broadcast TV stations. The easy way to buy TV time to sell your product nationally is to buy cable. That's what a lot of lazy people do. Buying five hundred local stations is a lot more time consuming than just buying a few cable networks for the same amount of time. But the results are well worth the effort.

CNN may claim they reach 60 million homes, but how many have tuned in to CNN at a specific time period? It would appear that everyone was watching CNN and nobody was watching any of the other hundred channels out there.

Local broadcast TV. It's cheaper, more effective, and it can work. At least it always has for me.

✓   Key Points

1.   Test your product on a small broadcast TV station. They're cheap and effective, and if the product clicks, slowly expand to other cities and other stations.

•

2.   Get in with a good telemarketing company. They'll supply you with 800 numbers, answer your calls, and do your "upselling" for you. I recommend West Telemarketing.

•

3.   Be careful what you say in your ad about when your product will arrive. Otherwise, you could be looking at FTC problems.

•

4.   Most people who enter the infomercial business lose their shirt. It's not as lucrative as it looks. It can be done, but you've got to be very careful and methodical in how you go about your business.

•

5.   Cable TV sounds like a good, cheap national buy but cable networks can use inflated, fudgy numbers. Stick with good ol' reliable, local broadcast TV, the cornerstone of my business since the 1950s.

CHAPTER **20**

Good Advertising

_____

Advertise: to call attention to things for
sale; to describe or praise publicly.

The art of advertising is based on the truism that catching
the public's attention is the first step toward selling a product.

I also believe in the value of getting people to notice—
now more than ever. In the proposed five-hundred-channel
era you've got to work much harder to stop people at your
advertisement when they're flipping the remote. Certainly
when I spray the GLH onto men's bald spots it's a great attention getter.

I've always been a big believer in directness. Humor is
great, but what do you remember afterward—your chuckle
or the product? Sometimes marketers have been able to combine both—as in that great ad for the Clapper, the product
that turns off the lights and stereo with just the clap of your
hands.

My marketing philosophy has always been simplicity:
Explain the problem, tell how my product is the solution,
how much it costs, and where to get it. That's what you

💡 MIRACLE BRUSH

"The magic lint remover that removes lint from velvets, wools, and flannels in seconds."

PROBLEM: *Lint.*

The Miracle Brush truly was a phenomenal product, and what was even more amazing about it is that I bought the item from our arch-enemy K-Tel, who found the product in Japan.

•

This was the only time in Ronco history that anything like this ever happened (sort of like Macy's and Gimbel's or McDonald's and Burger King working together), but I was in love with this product and saw great possibilities there.

•

What did the brush do? If you brush in a downward motion, it would pick up all the lint. To remove the lint from the brush, you brush it against your hand. You use this for suits, not sweaters.

•

K-Tel nabbed the rights to the Miracle Brush from a Japanese manu-facturer and K-Tel sold me their product. We both advertised on TV and both made a lot of money, which I guess helps explain why I would do business with K-Tel, a company famous for knocking off Ronco products after they became successful.

•

> We had a line of products and a lineup of retail accounts. Having access to the retail distribution allowed me to take their product, pay for television advertising, and reap the rewards.
>
> •
>
> In doing business with someone you don't like, or trust, if the money is big enough, you sometimes can overlook the personality conflicts. In fact, it was I who approached them about selling the brush, because I liked the way it functioned. My only regret is that I didn't find the manufacturer myself in Japan. But sometimes half a loaf is better than none.

should look at doing in your commercial or infomercial. Once you get past those most basic of points, then you can brainstorm for ways to get people's attention and make them remember your ad.

Does the windshield on your car fog up when it's cold outside? Are you prevented from seeing other cars, endangering your family? You present the problem in a question, and tell why you need such and such a product. *It will do this and that. It's inexpensive and easy to use. The problem won't occur anymore, your family won't be in an accident, this is where and how you can purchase it, this is the regular price and the TV discount price.*

In a classic 1960s newspaper ad to prospective clients, the New York agency Benton & Bowles posed six very important questions about the art of advertising and, in the process, summed up some great guidelines for my readers, ones that work just as effectively in infomercials as they do in traditional thirty-second TV spots or the print media:

1. Is there a big idea? *"Is it an important idea, such* as *Scope's 'medicine breath' or the positioning of Pledge furniture polish as a dusting aid?"*

2. Is there a theme line? *"A theme line that presents your selling idea in a memorable set of words can be worth millions of dollars of extra mileage to your advertising. Provocative lines like 'When E. F. Hutton talks, people listen," and "Please don't squeeze the Charmin" make it easy for the customer to remember your selling message. Incidentally, when you get a great one, treasure it and use it prominently in every print ad and television commercial you run."* (Or how about "Hey, good lookin', I'll be back to pick you up later" from the Mr. Microphone commercial. Or the Buttoneer's "The problem with buttons is they always fall off.")

3. Is it relevant? Advertising that is remembered—but the product forgotten—is deemed a failure. *"Jokes that steal attention from the selling idea, celebrities that have no logical connection with your product, and other irrelevancies can be devastating."*

4. Is it a cliché? *"Too much advertising is look-alike, sound-alike advertising. These advertisements are often costly failures."*

5. Is it believable? *"An advertisement can be totally truthful, yet sound unbelievable. Better to underpromise and be believable than to overpromise and lose credibility."*

(And finally, my favorite, which totally sums up my philosophy of advertising.)

6. Does it demonstrate? *"Nothing works harder or sells better than a demonstration of your product's superiority, especially in television. Look for every opportunity to demonstrate. Demonstrating—such as the simple exposition of how the Trac II razor works or the coating action of Pepto-Bismol—is the convincing way to sell.*

I have a different philosophy about infomercials than I do for standard one- or two-minute (short-form) TV commercials.

You do your basic sales pitch on TV in front of people. If you have a good product and the retail price is right, provided you have a reasonable cost for media, you should be successful. I don't believe in a high-tech production, just a basic, honest sales pitch—with mistakes and warts, if need be. I stuttered in one of my infomercials, and my producer wanted to edit it out, but I said leave it in. People do stutter when they're not scripted. And I think the audience responds better to a less slick presentation.

CHAPTER 21

When to Advertise and Infomercial Techniques That Really Work

The best time to advertise is when you can make money, whenever you can make a good deal. That said, I like weekends best because more people are at home. During the week I'm partial to late night, because people are laid back, relaxed, and often interested in buying product from television infomercials.

Direct response television often performs well in the early hours of the morning. The cost of airtime is cheapest then, and people's resistance is down.

But don't think the only time to buy time is weekends and late night. If you find that your product produces sales at seven A.M., take advantage of that. Test the different times of the day, and experiment with every time of the day to know where your market and profitability lie.

Time of the Year to Advertise

I like to concentrate my spending in the fourth quarter, because I'm a big believer in gifts. But we advertise products all year long. Life goes on, even without Christmas. People still buy gifts in the fall, spring, and summer.

Whether it's winter, spring, summer, or fall, anytime you can make a profit in a TV market, it's worth doing. Once again, one of the major components that dictates your profitability is the cost of media. TV is sometimes less expensive in the summer, but there are fewer people watching.

The One- or Two-Minute Direct Response Ad

For direct response television marketing, I prefer the full-length infomercial (twenty-eight minutes and thirty seconds) over a one- or two-minute short-form direct response commercial. The one-minute ads have limitations in the amount of sales and revenue you can generate. For instance, as a rule, it's too hard to direct-sell a product for more than $29.95 in a minute spot. Consumers just won't spend the money. They will on a half-hour infomercial because you can tell so much more of the story. You can touch on so many subjects and show why they should own your product. In a minute ad you have time to introduce your item, tell what it does and the problems it solves, the price, and how to order. In sixty seconds. It's very fast.

Buying Agencies

We have several people on staff whose daily job is to work with our twelve different buying agencies. We use the outside agencies to buy our TV time because that makes it easier for us to get better deals. We know that if we have more than one agency buying for us, we can get a better handle on comparative prices.

All the TV stations deal with most of the agencies, and they have only so much infomercial time in their inventory. It's very limited. They don't want to give it all to just one customer, so to be fair, they slice it up. And by working with so many agencies, we have that many more shots at the airtime.

For a company like mine that specializes in television marketing, the hardest thing to do is find reasonably priced airtime. We can never buy enough at a good price. You'll pay a commission (usually 12 percent) to the agencies, but if they can make you money, it's well worth it. Williams Television Time, run by Katie Williams, is the company I work with most often.

Per-Inquiry Marketing

For my bargains hunters out there, you may have heard about the per-inquiry (or PI) type of sales, where you pay the TV station on a per-order basis only. They run the commercial and you pay them for each order received. I'm not a big fan of PI marketing because you can't get enough of it.

The stations usually sell PI ads when they're having a difficult time moving their airtime inventory for cash, and only the weakest stations generally make PI deals. In a perfect world they'd much prefer selling you an ad for cash—it's much more lucrative. So naturally, if they could get cash out of you, they wouldn't be taking your PI business.

With a PI campaign you have no idea when your spots are going to run. It may be at four A.M. or six P.M. At six P.M. would be highly unlikely. The wee hours of the morning is usually more like it. What good is it doing for you being on at three A.M. on the weakest TV station in the market talking to three people? You're not going to be able to buy dessert with the money you can make in that time slot.

Better to pay cash where you have total control over where you'll be seen.

The serious dollars you'll make will come from paying cash rather than relying on PI, but it is possible to make money if you can get enough stations around the country to participate with you.

The one major drawback to PI: At the end of the week you will remit to the station the agreed-upon monies for each order taken. Suppose, after paying the station what you thought was due them, based upon the numbers you've received, you subsequently find out that you had a 5 percent credit card refusal and that another 6 or 7 percent returned the goods for a full refund: be aware that you'll have to absorb those losses.

Audiences

I'm a big believer in having an audience when you make infomercials. In fact, I think they're an essential part of the art form, just like playing to a crowd at the county fair. You need people responding to your product, asking questions, and being amazed. I don't hire shills, my audience has always truly been amazed at my products.

In Los Angeles it's easy to get audiences because tourists come to town all the time hoping to be on TV. We pay them $35 for being there all day and give them a lunch. Many want to trade their $35 for whatever product we might be marketing.

When I was in Chicago at Woolworth's and Maxwell Street, I would do all the talking. Now, I like to interact with my audience. I love getting testimonials, which, as any late-

THE RONCO ROLLERMEASURE

"It does jobs a tape measure can't!"

PROBLEM: *Tape measures are tough to use, especially when measuring floors and ceilings.*

The Ronco RollerMeasure was my alternative to the traditional tape measure. Most tape measures need two people: one at one end and the other at the other end. And it isn't very easy if you have to measure walls or rooms with curves.

•

The RollerMeasure is a perfect example of taking an old product and updating it with modern technology. The fact that my unit worked on curves was pretty great, and certainly enough to make the product worth marketing, but I went one step further. The RollerMeasure also happened to measure space with a digital counter, offering an accurate readout in feet and inches.

•

"An ordinary tape measure can tangle and often requires two people to hold it down. But not with the Ronco RollerMeasure. We designed the product with a three-foot handle so if you're doing a floor, the consumer doesn't have to get on his or her knees. And if you're doing a ceiling, you can do it without the use of a ladder. It also has a wheel on it, so you can roll it along the couch, around corners or over curves.

•

"Makes a great Christmas gift for carpenters and contractors, for interior decorators it's sensational, and it's great for landscapers too. If you sew, it makes all your measuring jobs so much easier. The perfect gift for everyone." One of our all-time classics.

night or Sunday-morning television fan knows, is an essential component of any infomercial. It tells the people at home that folks like them had success with the product.

The best testimonial I ever got was in the GLH infomercial, when, in the middle of the show, there was a man sitting in the second row who started shaking his head. Nancy Nelson, the hostess, went over to him, and he said, "I'm watching this, but you know what I think? I think that the people watching this infomercial are not going to believe what they see. But I'm sitting here and *I* can't believe what I'm seeing here. I'm telling you, folks, it's true. The man looks like he's got hair on his bald spot. I see it with my own eyes and it's true."

My infomercials are ad-libbed, because I couldn't write a script like that.

Not Available in Stores!

Hard as it may be to believe, I never once used those words in any of my ads, even though they were staples of some of my competitors' spots. There were some products I didn't put into retail initially, but I never talked about it on TV. And there was a good business reason why.

Let's say I put "Not available in stores!" in the commercial. And then the buyer for Wal-Mart calls, wants to buy 20,000 pieces of my product, and is willing to pay a premium to get it in stock. What do I say? The same thing any other sane businessman would say: "Sure. How soon would you like them delivered?"

Had I said, "Not available in stores," on TV and accepted the order from Wal-Mart, I would now have a major problem. A commercial on five hundred stations is saying you can't buy my product in a store. Now I have to change the commercial. And between the shipping back and forth between my agencies and the TV stations, the duplications, and the change in the ad itself, I could be looking at a bill between $50,000 and $100,000.

I've had good reasons not to sell some of my products at retail before (more on that in the retail chapter), but I always kept them to myself. I found it a lot easier to just not make retail deals—with the right to eventually end up there. I wouldn't want anyone saying to me, "Hey, Ron, you said the Pasta Machine wasn't available in stores. I saw it in a store."

All I have is my credibility. If I wasn't telling the truth about that, am I lying about something else? I wouldn't want to be put in that situation.

Asking for the Money

When making your infomercial, there's an art to how you ask your viewers to pick up the phone and order. You can throw out the 800 number as often as you'd like, but don't let it distract from the credibility of the product. Make sure you've sold your product thoroughly before you put your hand out and the 800 number is up on the screen.

I don't like to ask for money until I believe I have completely sold my prospective customers. In my infomercials we ask for money twice—two thirds of the way in and then again at the end. Figure that by the time you're 66 percent into the infomercial, you've really done your job. The last third of the infomercial is just reviewing and repeating what you've already said at the start. (This is for the people who use the remote control and have tuned in to your program in the middle rather than the beginning.)

If you were to ask for the money in the first quarter of the show, I believe consumers might make a determination that the product wasn't worth the money—not at your asking price. And once that negative thought is positioned in their minds, you can't get them back. Do it too early, and they'll say it's not worth it. They'll see more, you'll tell them about all the advantages of the product, but they've already decided. It's a negative, and it's hard to turn a negative around.

If You Agree to Tell a Friend

"I have the product that will solve the problem" (of bald spots), I said on the GLH infomercial. *"It's not $100, not $60, not $50, not even $40. And if you promise to tell a friend to help me get word of mouth, I'll sell it to you for $19.95."*

On the Food Dehydrator and GLH infomercials, I made viewers that special TV offer. Just spread the word and I would give them a deep discount. That was my way of giving them a bonus for buying from me today.

It's a lot more effective to give someone a reason for buying now, as opposed to "Here's the price." And my offer certainly made sense. Advertising costs a lot of money today. I'm sure many people said, "How will he know if I told a friend about his product?" I didn't. But most people are honest. I was pleasantly surprised when many people wrote to me, telling me how much they enjoyed the products, and adding that they did as I asked, and told a friend. So I know it had some effect in the marketplace.

Would I have given them the same price anyway? Of course. Was I misleading them? I don't think so. There was a logical reason for my request. Yes, I was hyping them, but it did accomplish my goal: extra sales and some free advertising.

Buy More than One

Whether you're on TV, demonstrating at fairs, or doing an appearance on a home shopping channel, always remember that the consumer who purchases your product may not be thinking about his or her future needs for gifts. We live in a society where people buy gifts for so many different days that are always ahead of us—Father's Day, Mother's Day, Valentine's Day, Christmas, birthdays, anniversaries, et cetera. And most people don't know what to get. So when you have the opportunity to talk to the consumer, devote some effort to selling an additional one or two products. You'll be surprised how many additional sales you can make by just reminding him or her to buy two or three—because they make great gifts. We always did that on the old Ronco TV ads.

All you have to do is ask.

Ancillary Marketing

Once you've got a successful product, you can look forward to the wonderful, lucrative world of ancillary marketing.

Jan Gildersleeve, a consultant for my company, came up with the great idea of contacting people who make products associated with pasta and having them participate in our marketing. One of her first moves when we decided to market the Pasta Machine was to set up a meeting at General Mills in Minneapolis. We had tested their flour with our machine and it worked well. We allowed them to test and use the product, and soon they wanted to work with us—to the tune of $100,000. All we had to do was use General Mills Gold Medal flour in our infomercial.

In essence, what General Mills really did was pay for much of the production of the infomercial up front.

Now, I didn't have to graduate college to know that if General Mills contributed $100,000, an olive-oil company would also find it worthwhile to participate. And they did. Bertolli olive oil kicked in $10,000 just to have their bottle on the TV screen. Prego, the spaghetti sauce company, also joined us, with a contribution. To date I have spent close to $20 million on local and national TV and have appeared on many major TV shows with the Pasta Machine. You'll always see a package of General Mills Gold Medal Flour or a bottle of Bertolli olive oil by my side. Because I delivered the promise. They got more than their money's worth and they're happy for it too.

Jan had a great idea in bringing these companies into our TV marketing. It was good for them, and it's good for us, and you can be sure we'll be doing a lot more of it in the future.

Ancillary Products

Once you've got a successful product, you can find or create many more items, not necessarily big products, to be marketed to your customer.

For instance, isn't it logical that after people bought the Food Dehydrator, they'd be interested in storage containers to put their dry food in? Storage containers aren't an exciting product, but people do have to store their food in something.

Once again, you can turn to an outbound telemarketing firm to handle the sales of these products. They'll work the phones and call your new customers. They're geared to the phone business and you're in business to supply your customers. You give them a piece of the profit, and the future possibilities are never ending.

Customer Service

We do all the customer service internally. I have twenty Ronco employees who do nothing else but solve problems and sell merchandise. The consumer today expects you to have an 800 number so he or she can call, ask questions, and get help. It's vitally important to have more than adequate staff in the customer service area. There's nothing worse than having a customer call with a question or a problem and just get a busy signal or no one answers the phone for five minutes. That customer will end up irate and will be more likely just to return the product to you or to the store for a refund. By having adequate numbers of customer service people, you'll not only solve a major problem but will also create another profit center for your company.

Every time customers call, you have another good reason to sell them another related product. You have them on the phone, and if they're happy with their purchase, and they usually are, you're able to sell them a whole variety of other products.

My customer service reps are very familiar with the products—they have them and use them at home. So when someone calls, they know how the product performs and are able to sell new related products that the company offers. For example our customer service staff now sells pasta mixes and other cooking items for Pasta Maker customers.

Name Selling

One of the mandates at Ronco, besides quality and innovation, is this: A name, address, and phone number are worth gold.

We always capture a telephone number in addition to the name and address of a customer, because those items are very, very valuable. One of the greatest assets of huge mail order firms like Fingerhut and Franklin Mint are the names of their customers. These are the people who year in and year out continue to buy their goods.

There are several list management firms who go to companies specializing in mail order such as Ronco and, on a yearly basis, buy the names of our customers. This, too, can be another great source of income to your new company.

Names are sold by the thousands, with the most recent customers being the most valuable—especially the ones who have purchased big-ticket items with a credit card. These companies like credit customers because it's easier to sell them products, they don't have collection problems, and, obviously, tend to have better credit ratings. And big-ticket customers tend to be upscale people with lots of money to buy goods.

Each name is usually worth around one dollar. We've been averaging hundreds of thousands a year for our customers' names. That's how lucrative the selling of names can be.

✓   Key Points

1.   Late night, weekends, and early morning are usually the best time to air infomercials.

•

2.   A one- or two-minute direct-response commercial will work if your product retails for under $30, but in most cases, the full-length infomercial is necessary for products with a higher price tag.

•

3.   Per-Inquiry marketing is a cheap way to get your ad on TV—no money down, usually, and you only pay for each order that the station generates. The only negative is you can't get enough airtime, so there are few sales.

•

4.   Ask for the order more than once in your infomercial, but wait until you're at least 60 percent through. Asking any earlier might turn off your customer and lose the sale, because you haven't given enough information to the consumer yet.

CHAPTER 22

The Home Shopping Revolution

Home shopping has been around since 1872, when Aaron Montgomery Ward of Chicago built the first great mail-order enterprise. At the time, most Americans still lived in rural settings, so there was a great opportunity to bring mass merchandising to the people. The mail-order catalog was rural America's main link to civilization.

By 1894 both Ward and his archrival Sears Roebuck offered mammoth "wish books," selling everything from farm equipment to couches and clothes. This is where America shopped until the 1920s, when more people started living in cities, and Ward and Sears compensated by building large chain stores nationally. Still, for the other half of the country who didn't live in the city, the huge catalog was the main way to shop for clothes, appliances, and other nonfood essentials.

Home shopping *was* the catalog business until the video revolution began with the introduction of television in 1946. Instead of leafing through a catalog, consumers could now see products demonstrated on TV. Sales opportunities were so much greater. You could tell and show so much more about a product on TV than with just a picture and advertising copy.

A lot of people think of me as TV's first pitchman, but that's not true. That honor has been credited to a man from Ohio named Bill Bernard, who in 1949 sold an early stainless steel blender called the Vitamix *("One of the most wonderful machines ever invented")* on television.

I came on the scene a few years later, but I did do one of the earliest infomercials, if not the first. I realized early on that I could buy television airtime cheaply on smaller stations, where station managers were more likely to sell me time in larger increments than the standard thirty-second or one-minute spot. To me this was gold, because if I had five minutes, as I once told an interviewer, "I could sell anything. Five minutes for me is a chance to mine gold."

Most of my ads for the Chop-O-Matic were the standard thirty-second and one-minute spots, but I also did several fifteen-minute versions on local stations, ads that ended with me saying, "Now here's your announcer to tell you how to order."

As we all know, back then, most shopping was done at retail stores and through catalog booklets. In the 1950s there were no limits on the amount of commercial time they could air, but the FCC soon clamped down. In 1984, during the Reagan era of relaxed government regulations, the FCC lifted the twelve-minute-per-hour limit on TV ads, and the infomercial era was born.

Victoria Principal, Ali MacGraw, and Cher carved out new careers as cosmetics hawkers; Susan Powter, a formerly overweight Dallas housewife, screamed, "Stop the insanity!" and became a household name; self-help gurus like Anthony Robbins became multimillionaires; and I came out of semi-retirement to find more success, via home shopping, than I

THE POPEIL POCKET FISHERMAN

"Want to make a boy happy?
Give him the Pocket Fisherman."

PROBLEM: *Fishing poles are too big and*
cumbersome; they're hard to travel with.

The Veg-O-Matic was my father's all-time best selling product. Close behind was the Pocket Fisherman. It didn't move as many units, but it won more hearts. People have a special fondness for a fishing pole that nine times out of ten was the first one they ever used.

•

The Pocket Fisherman was a small, collapsible fishing rod that attached to your belt; it could also fit in your car glove compartment. It was a great, functional gift for kids. Then, after the parents bought it, they would say, "Hey, this isn't such a bad idea. I've got to get one myself and keep it in the car."

•

There's nothing I love more in life than getting away from it all on my boat (which is named the *Pocket Fisherman)* with just a fishing rod in my hand. Can't say the same about my dad. He was not a fisherman, and he knew very little about the intricacies of fishing rods and reels.

•

He got the idea for the product from a customer, who suggested he try getting into the outdoor market, a business he and I had never really known existed. At the time, we had concentrated solely on the kitchen, the staple of the pitch business. The reasoning was that everyone has a kitchen and the homemaker spent a great deal of time there. Kitchen products were the true meaning of a mass market item. Then and now.

•

Most of our testing with the Pocket Fisherman took place at trout farms in the Chicago area, where we were always assured that the Pocket Fisherman would catch a fish.

•

As always, there was very little communication between my father and me, but he seemed to value my opinion. Dad worked with a team of engineers to put the product together and asked my thoughts about the various stages of development.

•

I thought it was unique. Did I ever think it would achieve the kind of success it did? No way. I really didn't know about the quantity of people in the country who were fishing addicts. Unless you're in the sporting goods business, you wouldn't have that kind of insight. Camping gear, fishing rods, backpacks, and all the gear that goes with campers is a huge business, one of the key reasons I decided to bring out my Food Dehydrator, to appeal to that crowd.

•

Even though I didn't think there would be much of a market for the Pocket Fisherman, I took it on, because I felt an obligation to show my father that he could always count on me to make sure that the maximum effort was exerted to make his products successful, even if I wasn't a big believer. I knew it was going to be a successful product, I just thought he was out of his mind for asking such a high price— $19.95, when I thought it should have sold for $9.99 tops.

•

Wherever I go, people talk to me about how much they loved the Popeil Pocket Fisherman. I was in a sporting goods store the other day, and the salesman told me he'd learned how to fish with it, not an uncommon comment. I got a kick out of watching the Robert Redford film *Sneakers,* where they used the Pocket Fisherman in their heist.

•

As of this writing, I am currently working on updating the Pocket Fisherman, and bringing it back to the marketplace, in a truly new and improved version, due to public demand.

•

"The Popeil Pocket Fisherman is so easy to cast. You don't have to be an expert to catch fish. It's fishing fun for the whole family, and only $19.95. What a gift!"

had ever achieved in all my years selling products strictly at retail. For instance, it took me ten years to sell 25 percent of what I sold in a year and a half with the Food Dehydrator infomercial. (They didn't win, but even Jerry Brown and Ross Perot ran for President via the infomercial. They wanted to go around the traditional media and straight to the people, and used the medium to raise money, ask for votes, and spread their toll-free 800 numbers.)

In the mid 1990s 101 million Americans were shopping from home, representing 55.2 percent of the adult population. Infomercials are a $1-billion-a-year business and there are those who are predicting it could increase to $10 billion by 1998. I personally doubt it, though, because of the expense of media versus the actual sales.

What does the infomercial do? It allows consumers to digest, in an entertaining form, an abundance of information about a product. It also allows them to purchase that product by just picking up their telephone and calling a toll-free number.

We used to just show the merchandise on TV and tell where to get it in thirty seconds or one minute. Now we have the opportunity to display the product and show, in an entertaining fashion, how it solves problems.

The infomercial business is really the mail order business, which didn't have any real credibility outside of rural areas until the late 1980s. The toll-free 800 telephone number, the growing acceptance of credit cards, and the money-back guarantee made the business what it is today. Mail order is a mass-market business, and many have made millions of dollars with it, myself included. But what few people realize today is that the golden era of infomercials—where you make big money directly from the TV marketing—is very much behind us.

I'm doing infomercials today solely because of the retail business I can achieve in stores. After an initial infomercial exposure of say, six months, my product is now presold and "as seen on TV."

It wasn't that way when I took the Food Dehydrator to television. I didn't do any retail at first. I made tens of millions of dollars just putting the product on television with my $33,000 infomercial. I spent more than $60 million advertising my product over a three-year period. That has to be some kind of record in the history of marketing one product.

One product with the same commercial. I don't think it's ever been done. Back in the sixties and seventies it was unheard of for a product to stick around this long, because retailers were always demanding a new product to bring customers into their stores.

If you can break even and make the public aware of your product via infomercials, retail buyers will want your product. If you could get your product in just a few of the major chains (Wal-Mart, Kmart, Sears, J. C. Penney, Target, Sam's Wholesale Club, B.J.'s, Costco, Montgomery Ward), you could make millions of dollars.

Others in the infomercial business have asked me to make commercials for their products, but I always decline. I enjoy developing my own product, and I also believe my marketing expertise would be somewhat watered down if, in fact, I were on twenty different commercials with twenty different products. It would appear that I was more of a spokesperson than a man who believed in a product that he created.

When you see an inventor on TV who's actually selling his own product, it has that extra punch of credibility, and that causes the consumer to go to the telephone or retail store and buy the product.

Shopping TV

Attention, shoppers! One home-shopping channel, QVC, did as much business in 1994—$1.2 billion, representing 56 million orders from viewers—as the entire infomercial industry did that same year. The industry, which has been growing at a rate of 20 percent a year, dialed up a whopping $2.5 billion in sales. That's a whole lot of cubic-zirconia rings, silver bracelets, pasta machines, and food dehydrators. And industry forecasters only see home shopping getting bigger and bigger, with some enthusiastic proponents going as high as $100 billion by the year 2000 (as compared to the retail dollars of $600 billion!)

When General Publishing went on QVC to sell a twenty-fifth-anniversary book celebrating CBS's *60 Minutes* TV show, their entire supply sold out in seventeen minutes. That was 8,000 books, worth $240,000 in sales. And the author, Frank Coffey, didn't have to personally visit one bookstore. Not a bad way to sell a product. And when QVC host Bob Bowersox, a former actor and restaurant owner, went on QVC to sell his first cookbook, *In the Kitchen with Bob,* he sold a record 155,000 copies over a twenty-four-hour period, becoming a candidate for the fastest-selling book in history.

And it's not just books. Gold chains, diamond rings, pasta machines, camcorders, designer sweaters and dresses, food dehydrators, costumed dolls, autographed baseballs, spray-on vitamins, the latest CDs by *Entertainment Tonight*'s John Tesh, Ivana Trump's perfumes, Marie Osmond's dolls, and Tony Little's exercise equipment—these are the sorts of goods that have been selling on the home shopping channels, and over the years, experts see just about everything else in the retail universe being marketed as well.

The catalog industry was doing $60 billion in sales in the early 1990s, but listen to this: It took catalog pioneer L.L. Bean eighty-one years to hit the billion-dollar mark in sales; QVC (which stands for Quality, Value, and Convenience) began in 1986 and crossed over the billion-dollar mark six years after its debut. As of this writing QVC is the world's largest electronic retailer, with 4 million home viewers who are always in the mood to shop. Its nearest competitor, the Home Shopping Network, had sales of $1 billion in 1993. The size of QVC's cable audience is nearly double that of HSN.

In the beginning home shopping was seen by many as a

downscale medium whose average viewer was a far cry from the sophisticated urban upscale consumer that merchants try to reach. That was the original focus, but not anymore. *Business Week* reported a 1994 study showing that the TV shoppers of today are, in fact, young, well educated, reasonably affluent, fashion conscious, and not exclusively women. (Some 48 percent of TV shoppers were men, as opposed to 47 percent of the retail shopping population.)

Home shopping, at its core, is the catalog for the video generation. Why bother reading when you can watch TV? Consumers who buy from catalogs and direct mail are prime candidates for TV shopping because of their previous track record—they already buy products without inspecting them first. In a catalog, a picture and some ad copy are all that's needed to make them part with their money. Think of how many more pieces of product could be moved if they could actually see the product being demonstrated on television.

Home shopping channels, like catalogs, are great for the elderly or disabled consumers for whom a trip to the store is difficult. They're also quite popular in rural areas, where the nearest shopping mall is probably several miles away, and are a nice urban alternative to shoppers who are sick of the safety issues now associated with visiting the city shopping mall.

While shopping channel sales are still dwarfed by print catalogs, their selling power is incredible. One day on QVC we took in $1.2 million in twelve minutes for my Pasta Machine and set an all-time record for dollars sold per minute. A few hours later that day I sold another $1 million worth of the same product, but not in twelve minutes. This time it took half an hour.

And I'm not the only one to experience the phenomenon of instant QVC megasales. Former Fox CEO Barry Diller became an investor in QVC after hearing about it from his friend, designer Diane Von Furstenberg. She had taken a field trip to QVC's headquarters in West Chester, Pennsylvania, and watched soap opera star Susan Lucci pitch a hair product carrying her name and move $450,000 worth of goods in an hour. She told Barry Diller and he was hooked.

The first home shopping channel was the aptly titled Home Shopping Network, which began in 1982, founded in St. Petersburg, Florida, by real estate developer Roy Speer and radio man Lowell "Bud" Paxson. A lawyer at first who made his fortune in real estate, Speer invested in a number of businesses in the 1970s, including a news-talk radio station in Clearwater, Florida, WWOT. When an advertiser went bankrupt in 1977 and couldn't pay his bill with cash, Speer's holdings grew to include a crate of electric can openers.

What to do with 112 can openers? WWOT station manager Paxson came up with the idea of selling them over the air. After the first crate sold out, Speer bought another, and another. He quickly came to the realization that he could make more money selling gadgets to listeners than airtime to advertisers. Branching into other housewares, and then ceramic collectibles, the radio sales feature soon had a name— *The Bargaineers*—and began to dominate the WWOT broadcast day.

In 1982 Speer and Paxson—to whom he'd given an interest in the home shopping business—renamed the program the *Home Shopping Club* and put it on local cable TV. Annual sales soon shot into the millions. The *Home Shopping Club* made its national debut in 1985, and by 1986 annual sales reached $160 million, then $730 million in 1988 and crossed the $1 billion mark in 1991.

Joseph Segal, who made a fortune with the Franklin Mint, joined the Home Shopping Wars in 1986. The Pennsylvania financier came upon HSN after reading their prospectus for investors. He then watched HSN on the air and hated what he saw. "I thought it was horrible," Segal told *The New York*

Times. He didn't care for HSN's cheap and tacky sets, or the arm-twisting sales pitches.

So instead of investing in HSN, he hired experienced TV executives, raised $30 million, and founded his own home shopping channel: QVC. Segal's product line was affordable, but more upscale than HSN's, focusing on brand names and designer clothes. Rather than push products, his hosts would simply explain them. And once they were introduced, products would be assigned catalog numbers and made available twenty-four hours a day. QVC quickly surpassed HSN's sales and audience reach.

Still, both channels focus on many of the same things: clothing, cosmetics, kitchen products, and jewelry. Viewers write down the channel's phone number, product stock number, and price, which are flashed on screen, call the 800 number, and order direct.

Besides convenience, the home shopping channels also sell at a discount. Because they move products in such a huge volume, their prices are often equal to or lower than what consumers would pay in stores. (There is still shipping and handling, which can add a small amount to the bill. Still, you save local sales tax, and you don't have to go to the store, search for a parking space, and deal with crowds, only to find out your product is out of stock. Shopping from television is much easier.)

One of the reasons QVC sells more products than HSN, in my opinion, is that QVC has some of the greatest salespeople as hosts that I've ever come in contact with. Steve Bryant, Bob Bowersox, and Mary Beth Roe continue to hold my admiration for their innate abilities in selling a wide variety of products. What makes them unique is that they can sell *anything.* I don't put myself in their league.

The great thing about QVC or HSN is that no matter what is happening in the world, products are always being sold. There are some people who don't want their regular programming interrupted by the O. J. Simpson trial or Gulf War coverage. They want escape, and QVC offers plenty of it, twenty-four hours a day.

As of this writing, QVC's peak selling day was January 24, 1993, when the network took in $19 million in one day! The occasion was the 145th anniversary of the discovery of gold at Sutter's Mill, California, an event QVC commemorates annually with an all-gold-jewelry day that features fourteen-karat pieces for an average of $90 per unit.

Home Shopping is obviously a great business. That's why virtually every major retailer, after initially shunning it, has discussed plans to launch their own shopping channels. Shrinking leisure time and the swelling ranks of women in the work force mean fewer people have the time for a nice, leisurely shop, and many people simply hate the experience of shopping at crowded department stores and malls. For network owners, they have a low-cost distribution system, they don't need thousands of stores or thousands of pieces of inventory that are scattered all across the country, and they don't need to hire thousands of employees. Just a small group of executives, phone operators, people to work in the shipping area, and quality TV hosts.

They Like "As Seen on TV" Too

One of your ultimate goals in your TV marketing campaign should be to get your product on a home shopping channel like QVC or HSN. This is where I make my serious money.

Not everybody can get in the door to sell their product to the buyers at the home shopping channels, whose concerns aren't any different from those of the buyers at Kmart or Wal-Mart. They want presold goods that have been heavily marketed on television.

So if you've been out there plugging away with infomercials and/or commercials, chances are good that the home shopping networks will have seen your ads on TV and will be interested in carrying your product.

Does your product have to be successful? Not necessarily. If you can just get on the air and break even for six months in an infomercial, you will create enough exposure so that QVC and retail stores will take you on, and then, hopefully, the money will really begin to pour in. Retailers want products to have national TV exposure. QVC is a national cable network. Getting your product with a national audience will help you get into retail.

When home shopping began, it was viewed as the last stop on the retail journey, the place to unload a variety of inexpensive merchandise that might be deemed unsalable by any other means. Obviously that's all changed. If you sell your product on QVC, you can't also sell on HSN or any other cable shopping network, and vice versa. As long as they deem you to be a "celebrity," you're exclusive. When they know you're successful with them, and that you have a quality product, they want to keep you in the confines of their marketplace, and they have the power because of the large quantity of product they're capable of ordering from you. Certainly I would do the same thing if I were in their shoes.

The shopping channels like to have a normal retail markup. They call it "keystone," which is 50 percent of the regular retail price. However, they do offer their customers special discounted prices where their markup might be as low as 33 percent rather than 100 percent.

Like a retailer they buy the product outright from me and then resell it to the public. If all goes well, they'll reorder more. If you're lucky, you get to come on the air and sell your creation, and that's when sales really take off.

If I didn't go on the air plugging my products, I'm confident that QVC's hosts and hostesses would do a fine job selling my goods, and that they would continue reordering merchandise. That said, I believe sales might only be 20 percent of what they are today. This is due, in part, to the minimal time allotted to airing a given product. When I participate personally, I'm granted much more time to make a pitch.

It's not just that my exposure helps move the merchandise, but because I've taken the time to fly to their studio in West Chester, Pennsylvania, they devote more airtime to me. If your product is just another in a line of goods, you'll get maybe three or four minutes. But when I come on as a spokesman for my product, they usually devote around fifteen minutes to me. With more time you can tell so much more about your products, and sales are more substantial. It's like the difference between a thirty-second commercial and a half-hour infomercial.

But as with anything else, you have to walk before you run, and hopefully you'll find a way to be invited to come on a home shopping channel personally to talk about your product. It might not happen the first time. You might need some media exposure, print or TV or a combination of both, to make it happen. Whatever you do, work on making it happen, because it will pay off with sales.

Home Shopping Icing

At one time the infomercial business was one of the easiest in the world. Now we're lucky to break even or make a few dollars. When I say a few dollars, we gross between $50,000 and $100,000 a week on our infomercials, and that's gross profit dollars. That includes the cost of goods and media time, which are the two major expenses at my company, but doesn't factor in overhead and tooling amortization.

That's why the serious money to be made today is at retail. Home shopping is icing on the cake. Still, you can't lose going on QVC or Home Shopping Network. If you have a reasonably good product at a fair price, you will make money. You don't have to spend anything to get on, and you get millions of dollars' worth of free advertising time that sells product for you in other areas, like retail and outbound telemarketing.

How to Get Your Product on a Home Shopping Channel

So now you're sitting there thinking about how nice it would be to just bypass the infomercial and retail process, make your life simple, sell your product to a shopping channel and watch the profits pour in? Stand in line.

Most likely, you won't even get a meeting with a buyer. You will, however, get it after they've seen your product on TV. *Remember, they want preadvertised merchandise.*

But there are ways to get in there, even if your product isn't preadvertised. QVC and HSN sells products all day long, and they're always looking for something new to offer their viewers. After all, they can't just show the same jewelry and clothing every day.

Now, it helps if you know someone, but the networks also have "Vendor Relations" departments that anyone can call for information. Give them a ring, and get a product-information form from them. Fill it out, attach a photo (samples are discouraged), and hope for the best. Still, this is a real long shot. At HSN, according to *Inc.,* buyers process 1,100 product sheets a week and 75 percent fail to make the first cut. On the other side of the coin, 25 percent get called in for the second audition. That's a foot in the door. Maybe the first product won't make it, but when you come up with the second one, at least you have an exec's name you can call on next time.

☼ THE RONCO AUTO-CUP

"How would you like to drink a hot cup of coffee on your way to work?"

PROBLEM: *Spilled or cold coffee.*

There's nothing like driving to work with a hot cup of coffee in your hand. Nine times out of ten it's gonna spill on you. The automakers have helped solve the problem with in-dash cup holders, but back in the 1960s, when I came up with the Ronco Auto-Cup, Detroit's minds were on other things.

●

Back then, when commuters commuted with coffee, it was impossible to drink the beverage without having it splatter all over them. That's where I came in with the Ronco solution.

●

The Auto-Cup was a no-spill cup with a small hole in the lid to drink through. A spring lid sealed the hole after use, and even shaking couldn't force the coffee out. You could turn it upside down and it wouldn't leak out.

●

The problem was solved and we sold over 1 million of the cups.

●

"The portable no-spill cup that keeps drinks hot or cold. This specially designed double-walled insulated cup lets you drink hot coffee or tea on your way to work or anywhere. Just press the lever and drink. An ideal gift for anyone who's on the move."

So if at first you don't succeed, keep trying. Some 3,100 vendors, about 100 of whom are new to the network in any given month, offer their goods to QVC viewers. "The key to retailing electronically is fresh, exciting merchandise," a QVC exec told *Inc.* "We have the ability to use up merchandise very quickly."

QVC says that once their merchandise buyer evaluates your "Product Data Sheet," they will get back to you in three weeks. Here's how they explain the process of getting on air: "If your product is appropriate for QVC, a sample will be requested. This sample must pass our rigorous Quality Assurance requirements. Once a sample has been approved, we will arrange to develop a plan to work with your product. All product received by QVC must be individually packaged, labeled, and shipped directly to our warehouse in accordance with QVC regulations. This ensures our seven-to-ten-day delivery guarantee to our customers. Once the product has been processed through our Quality Assurance stage and assigned a warehouse location, your product is ready to be programmed for television."

And what type of product is QVC looking for? "A wide variety of unique, quality goods that can be demonstrated on air. Exclusive product launches and products offered for the first time are always of interest. Our programming is thematic. Product selections are considered based upon how they will segment into our broadcast programs."

The products QVC won't sell are junior apparel, furs and fur-related products, guns and gun-related products, subscriptions, personalized items, 900 phone programs, and service-related products. As far as the QVC demographic, the network targets thirty-five- to fifty-year-old men and women with annual incomes of $40,000 plus. "They are established homeowners who shop from catalogs and other direct-mail vehicles."

Some of the questions they'll ask you on the Product Data sheets:

Apparel & Accessories: QVC wants to know the suggested retail price, the selling price to QVC, features/benefits, fiber content, color availability, monthly production capability, quantity available on hand, catalog and/or retail stores currently carrying the product, whether the product ever appeared for sale on TV.

Health & Beauty: Choose the product category that best describes the product (skin care, color, fragrance, personal care) and then describe its unique selling features. Additionally, QVC wants to know what kinds of tests have been made for the product, what claims can be made about it, and whether it has been patented. If there's a product spokesperson, you need to send in a head shot, bio, and three-to-five minutes of video footage.

Jewelry: Here's where you describe the target consumer market, cite your approximate yearly volume, say whether the product has ever appeared on television, and check what kind of jewelry you plan to sell: sterling silver, base metal, genuine stones, synthetic stones, 18K, 14K, or 10K.

Another way to get in the door is via an agent (not much different from the traditional "rep"). They deal with the home shopping networks on a regular basis and can shop your product. For a commission on sales your agent can present your product to a buyer, usher it through quality control, track it into the warehouse, train the host, script the presentation, and decorate the set. (Obviously you'll make a lot more money and be in better control of your destiny by doing it yourself.)

Once the home shopping channel says yes to your product, the testing process begins again, and I'm not talking about product testing. With new products, they sometimes

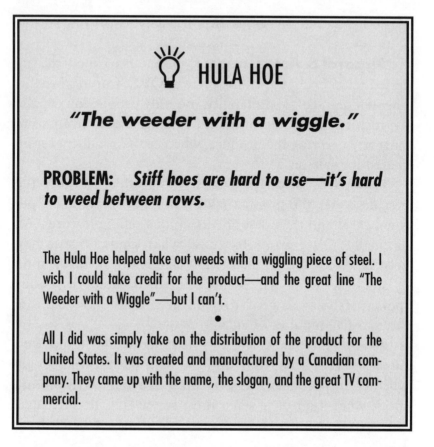

💡 HULA HOE

"The weeder with a wiggle."

PROBLEM: *Stiff hoes are hard to use—it's hard to weed between rows.*

The Hula Hoe helped take out weeds with a wiggling piece of steel. I wish I could take credit for the product—and the great line "The Weeder with a Wiggle"—but I can't.

•

All I did was simply take on the distribution of the product for the United States. It was created and manufactured by a Canadian company. They came up with the name, the slogan, and the great TV commercial.

run a marketing test in the middle of the night to get a feel for demand. If you pass that hurdle, they'll then decide how many they can sell, order exactly that, and schedule your product's first appearance. Initial orders vary. For the Pasta Machine, their first order was for 15,000 pieces. Keep in mind, the infomercial for the Pasta Machine had been on TV for about six months prior to QVC. Approximately $5 million had already been spent on airtime. It was for that reason that the order was as high as it was.

💡 THE POPEIL BAGEL CUTTER

This one I can take credit for. I got the idea after my girlfriend cut her finger one morning slicing a bagel. It occurred to me that if you surrounded a bagel with a piece of plastic, you could steady your hand.

•

The product not only prevents you from cutting your hand when you cut a bagel but it has slats, which allows you to quarter a bagel so it will fit in your toaster. That unit is sold at retail, while the basic product (no slats) is given away with the Pasta Machine, since the Pasta Machine also makes bagels.

Celebrity Partners

A lot of people have been making deals with celebrities to help sell their products. Victoria Principal, Ali MacGraw, and Cher have all become cosmetics queens. Vanna White sells tooth polish. Judy Norton-Taylor of *The Waltons* sells Dianetics books. Dionne Warwick pushes her psychic advice line.

The problem with celebrity endorsements is that now you're selling the celebrity, not the product. At one time, seeing celebrities on TV promoting a product was a novelty. Now we're all used to it.

The kinds of celebrities who go on TV today are ex–film stars and TV actors, and each has his or her own following. But so what if Engelbert Humperdinck came on to sell a food slicer? If you didn't like Engelbert and the way he sang songs, would you care about his food slicer? Probably not. He's not known for his food-slicing abilities. If he were there to sell a compilation of his greatest hits, the price was right, and you liked his stuff, you might buy it. That would make more sense. For a product to really move with a celebrity endorsement, the product should be associated with his or her past.

At least with the cosmetics, having actresses selling them sometimes makes sense. They're beautiful, and what are they selling? Beauty. Endless youth. Glamour. But not always.

Raquel Welch, Dolly Parton, Loni Anderson, Linda Evans, Joan Collins, Susan Anton, Donna Mills, Stefanie Powers, Jane Seymour, Morgan Brittany, and Farrah Fawcett are just a few of the actresses who did beauty infomercials that were acknowledged as bombs.

"We spent a lot of time and money on an infomercial with Joan Collins for Bioflora, a skin-care product," Kevin Harrington, the executive vice-president of National Media told *Women's Wear Daily.* "It taught us that it's difficult just putting a celebrity's name on something if the person is not wholeheartedly behind the product."

So don't think cutting a deal with a celeb to sell your product is a shortcut that will get you that much closer to instant riches. The star usually wants a big cut of the profits, as well as a handsome check for his or her day's work on the infomercial. Big stars can command as high as $1 million advances, plus 1 to 5 percent of the gross sale, while lesser names pull in anywhere from $30,000 to $100,000, plus a cut.

I think you can be much more effective just focusing on the product. Your profits, in the end, will be much greater.

Returns

Both HSN and QVC will accept any merchandise returned within thirty days. Some 20 percent of the merchandise sold on TV is usually returned, which is huge, when compared to the 3 percent return rate of traditional retail outlets, but about on a par with catalog merchandise. (I try not to give credit on returns to any of my retail customers, but only replacement. In that way I do not lose my profit margin on any returned goods.)

The returns are part of the cost of doing business, and well worth it. I believe the fact that consumers can readily return their home shopping merchandise is what built QVC and HSN into credible forces. Consumers don't view them as fly-by-night outfits; they trust buying from them, just like they trust Sears and Wal-Mart.

Fulfillment Houses

In setting up your new home shopping business you're probably thinking that you can sit at home, answer the phone, ship the products out yourself, and become an instant millionaire. Wrong. Let the professionals do what they do.

A fulfillment house is necessary. They have the computer equipment to keep track of your product. When someone calls and says, "What happened to my package?" they have the ability to know when it was sent out, where it is today, and when it will get to the customer. Sure, you could do that, too, but you'd have to buy a lot of computer hardware and hire a lot of people to do the job effectively.

Some fulfillment houses do a variety of jobs: they'll open your mail, deposit your money, ship your goods, and keep track of returns. You can expect the fulfillment house, in most cases, to charge a fee of $1 or $2 a package. (Obviously it's going to cost a lot more to ship a NordicTrack than a can of GLH.)

United Parcel Service is everywhere, and every major city has several fulfillment houses; they're usually listed in the Yellow Pages. Even if you're doing your TV marketing test in the Midwest and you're in California, you want to get a fulfillment house close to home—not in the Midwest. That way you can keep closer tabs and help get the product to the house.

What to do if you're really starting small, think you'll just be sending out one or two hundred pieces of product for your test, and really want to do it yourself? You just want information from the Rockford test before deciding how to proceed? Say on your commercial that your product will be out in four to six weeks, and after a week of advertising, you'll have plenty of time to make a quick deal with a fulfillment house. If you don't get that many orders, you won't have to make a deal, and you can ship out the fifty to one hundred pieces of product yourself and move on.

Catalog Marketing

When it comes to the home shopping revolution, a lot of would-be entrepreneurs think of catalogs as a nice alternative to infomercials. True, catalog marketers like L.L. Bean and Lands' End have a very good business, but for most people, you might as well drill for oil. You'd probably do much better there than in starting your own catalog business.

My first question to you as a catalog marketer would be: how many products are you going to put in it? Fifty? Where are you going to get fifty different products from? . . . Fifty different manufacturers? How many are you going to order of each product? You don't want to put it into your catalog without having it in your warehouse, so you'd better be prepared to order a lot. What's your staff going to be like, to purchase the products and keep track of them? Where are you going to get your mailing lists from? Why does someone want your catalog over someone else's? Can you deal with taking orders from credit cards as well as checks? What kind of policy do you have for returns? It costs a lot of money to print up catalogs, and for the postage to send them out. Are you prepared for that?

It can be done, by the newcomer with substantial net worth, who understands the business, who's made his or her living via mail order, but for the average guy on the block who wants to go into the business, it's just not going to happen. He'll lose his shirt—as opposed to the guy who takes his invention to the fair, rents a booth, sells it, and does well enough to be able to pay for a small TV marketing campaign on a few local broadcast TV stations. He can work his way all the way up to infomercials, home shopping channels, and retail stores to make real big-time money.

Why Home Shopping Took Off

A question I get all the time is "Ron, why do you think people like to watch jewelry and other goods being sold on TV? Isn't that boring?" Not necessarily. In the wee hours of the morning, when the same movies are being shown over and over, and viewers have the opportunity to look at something new, a great variety of products, they find this stuff fascinat-

💡 MR. DENTIST

"The easy way—for healthier gums and teeth."

PROBLEM: *You get to have shiny teeth only a few times a year—after a visit to the dentist.*

I was way ahead of my time with this product, which I conceived of myself, when I set out to take the same teeth-cleaning technology used by dentists into the home.

●

"Your dentist doesn't polish your teeth with a toothbrush—why should you?" I said in the commercial. Dentists use what appears to be a rubber or soft plastic tip that rotates to polish your teeth and give you that perfect smile. Mr. Dentist did the same thing, on a smaller scale, with a motor-driven tool that fit in your hand. Just apply some regular toothpaste, and you looked marvelous.

●

My daughter Shannon was in the commercial, along with a lot of friends—even the waitress who worked at one of my favorite delis—Nate-n-Al's of Beverly Hills.

●

Now why do I believe that I was ahead of my time with Mr. Dentist? Very simply, today, there are so many battery-operated toothbrushes available. Mr. Dentist was the forerunner of all of them.

●

"Mr. Dentist—massages gums and polishes teeth gently, effectively, effortlessly."

ing. Remember, we're a nation of shoppers. We love to shop. That's what we do.

I also think the shopping channels were very smart to hire hosts and hostesses. They have developed a relationship with their viewers. Many of them turn on their TV sets just to watch and listen to their friendly hosts and possibly communicate by calling and talking on the air with them. Viewers like the hosts, they like to shop, and the two seem to be intertwined.

Home shopping took off initially because of the novelty. It wasn't much different from me starting in TV in the 1950s with the Chop-O-Matic and making a splash. Back then you could sell most anything via television because we had a captive audience and there was minimal competition. TV advertising time was cheap and there was the novelty of buying something that you saw on TV.

The shopping channels took advantage of all the people with insomnia who couldn't get to sleep. The programming wasn't that great at first, but showing a different product every five minutes kept the viewer's attention because there was always something new just around the corner.

Another thing. Women *love* jewelry. They love to wear it, talk about it, shop for it, and watch it on TV. HSN and QVC played into their love affair. Go put a bookmark here right now and turn on QVC or HSN. I guarantee you'll see jewelry being sold. Nine times out of ten that's what's being marketed. As I was writing this paragraph, I turned on the TV to see if my theory was correct. What I found was rings on QVC, a bracelet on HSN, and earrings on the Shop at Home channel.

I often ask myself: Will the American female consumer ever get tired of jewelry? I'm convinced the answer is no. Will the channels tire of jewelry? No way. A) It sells, B) there are high margins, and C) it's a small product that doesn't take up a lot of space in the warehouse and it's inexpensive to ship or mail to the customer. And that's very important.

It's funny, but if you look back at the old Sears catalogs of the 1800s, they don't appear to be that different from the current infomercial and home shopping TV shows. An 1892 Sears catalog, for instance, is almost totally devoted to jewelry and watches, along with fifty-five pages of excerpts from testimonial letters.

So why haven't I gotten involved in the jewelry racket? It's too competitive. I don't like products with too much competition. One of the criteria when I create a product is to make sure there's not a jillion in the marketplace. I look for products that haven't successfully been marketed on television, like pasta machines and food dehydrators.

The Future of Home Shopping

Bill Gates, the $3 billion Microsoft software wonder, once gave *Fortune* his vision of the future of shopping. "You're watching *Seinfeld* on TV, and you like the jacket he's wearing. You click on it with your remote control. The show pauses and a Windows style drop-down menu appears at the top of the screen, asking you if you want to buy it. You click on yes. The next menu offers you a choice of colors; you click on black. Another menu lists your credit cards, asking which one you'll use for this purchase. Click on MasterCard or whatever. Which address should the jacket go to, your office, or your home, or your cabin? Click on one address and you're done—the menus disappear and *Seinfeld* picks up where it left off.

"Just as you'll already have taught the computer about your credit cards and addresses, you will have had your body measured by a 3-D version of supermarket scanners, so the system will know your exact sizes. And it will send the data electronically to a factory, where robots will custom-tailor the jacket to your measurements. An overnight courier service will deliver it to your door the next morning. And because this system cuts out so many middlemen, the jacket will cost 40 percent less than the off-the-rack version you'd find in a department store."

Will this day really arrive? With cable TV and telephone companies investing billions of dollars to provide cities and towns and suburbs with two-way data communications, major interactive shopping seems to be inevitable. After all, it's just a high-tech extension of direct marketing—selling to consumers through catalogs, infomercials, or home shopping channels.

I've heard some people predict that by the year 2000, nobody will shop at retail anymore; that all purchases will be made via TV or computer. To them I say baloney. That's like saying, years ago, that when movies went on TV, people would stop going to movie theaters or that, more recently, video would hurt the movie business. But as you can see, the theaters are full and the video stores are doing big business.

Home shopping will never replace the retail business. There's still a great segment of the population that likes to see and feel what a product looks like before they plunk down their cash. Even though money-back guarantees are prevalent in the mail-order home-shopping business, many just find it easier to stop down to the mall to buy, instead of having to repack an item later and send it back.

I believe that QVC and HSN will continue to dominate the TV shopping arena, and that some of the new channels being developed by retailers, mail order houses, and even QVC and HSN themselves *(TV Macy's,* Time Warner and Spiegel's *Catalog 1, Q2,* for younger QVC viewers, and HSN spin-off *TSM)* may pick up a little business, but mostly at the expense of their current customers.

What I do see in the future is all of the shopping channels dropping their exclusivity provisions and selling the same products. You can sell a hell of a lot more product nonexclusively than you can exclusively. QVC's and HSN's loyal viewers will stick with their channels, but the other shopping channel competitors remaining will fight for a tiny sliver of what's left.

Some Home Shopping Presentation Tips

Some things to remember when selling your products on a home shopping channel:

- Make merchandise seem special, limited, and available now.
- If selling clothing, choose apparel in primary colors. Complicated patterns look fuzzy on TV. Additionally, stock up on large sizes. Many home shoppers are women who wear size 14 and up.
- Describe scenarios in which viewers might use the merchandise: "Perfect for cruises," "A great present," et cetera.
- Sell merchandise with features that are easy to demonstrate, such as cameras, vacuum cleaners, and kitchen appliances.
- I don't believe in this for infomercials, but for a home shopping network, it's not a bad idea to work with a celebrity, who can help glamorize your product. In my case, I'm lucky that the celebrity for my product is me. I've been around for so long, and have spent so many millions of dollars of advertising for TV, that I'm now a celebrity.
- Develop a good rapport with your on-air hosts. Home viewers respond to your interplay. QVC often gives viewers the opportunity to talk on air with hosts and celebrity guests (hopefully that will be you one day) as well as participate in games and win prizes.

✓ Key Points

1. A good infomercial campaign—even if your product isn't a big hit—can get you on a home shopping channel. They like preadvertised products.

•

2. You can call "Vendor Relations" at the home shopping channels directly to submit your product for review. The odds are against you—since hundreds of others are doing the same thing—but you never know. If you have a product that's new, innovative, and fits into what the channel is looking for, you might be invited to sell your product.

•

3. A lot of marketers use celebrities to help sell their products. You'll make a lot more money, and be in business a lot longer, if you just focus instead on your product, and not a celebrity crutch.

•

4. Don't ship the goods out yourself—give the job to the professionals at a fullfillment house.

CHAPTER **23**

A Day in the Life at QVC

I'm sure people who watch me on QVC think I jump into a limo, get escorted to the green room (where celebrities and guests hang out prior to their appearance), and when it's my turn to come on, just walk onstage, do my demonstration, talk with the host or hostess, rack up $1 million in sales, and then leave.

I wish it were that simple.

A trip to West Chester, Pennsylvania, to visit QVC takes a good deal of preparation. Let me tell you exactly what goes into it.

I begin by hopping a plane from the West Coast to Philadelphia at 6:45 A.M. with my associate, Mike Srednick. Mike is with me to interact with the QVC exec. He works with them for scheduling and product ordering and basically deals with any problems they or I may have. He communicates with them regularly.

It's now about five P.M. At the airport we rent a car or my

💡 CELLUTROL

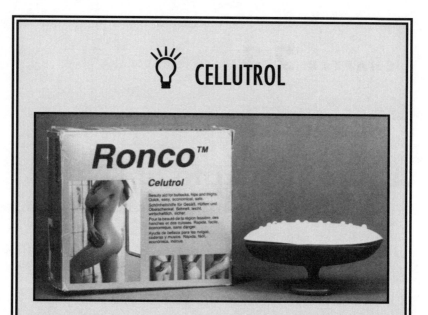

"The beauty aid for buttocks, hips, and thighs"

PROBLEM: *Cellulite.*

Cellutrol is another example of my introducing a less expensive, mass market alternative to a problem.

•

I knew that the problem of cellulite—the little wrinkles that women get in their thighs—was a serious one for the American female consumer. There was a product in the marketplace being sold in fine department stores. Stores like Bloomingdale's and Neiman Marcus sold it at top prices, and they moved a lot of product.

•

I attempted to create a product that would do basically the same thing, but for considerably less money. And instead of selling it at department stores, I sold it through drug chains, where consumers were accustomed to buying inexpensive beauty products.

•

Cellutrol was a massage type glove that had a compartment to hold ivy extract soap, which you could continue to order separately. (Again, the principle of the razor blade business.) It wasn't that much different from the product being sold at the department stores, it just cost much less to buy.

•

This was a new market segment for me, but not for long. Cellutrol had a very short shelf life. A few months into the marketing and further research, I discovered that nothing gets rid of cellulite except possibly exercise, and I even have my doubts about that.

•

This made me really uncomfortable and I stopped marketing the product. As I look back today, Cellutrol is one of the products I wish I had never gotten involved with. I was bamboozled into thinking that because the better department stores carried such an item at such high prices, the product had to work.

•

These kinds of products leave a bad taste in my mouth, because they're duping the consumer, who in turn may end up not being a future customer for myself and others who take pride in bringing the consumer products that really do the job.

brother Steve picks us up, and we drive about thirty miles to West Chester.

An hour later, we stop at the supermarket, where I hand-select, personally, each vegetable and fruit we will be displaying for the Ronco Electric Food Dehydrator. Since the machine makes beef jerky and dries assorted vegetables and fruits, we need everything from kiwi and mangos to a variety of the more common fruits, vegetables, and meats.

By this time the basket is full, and we start to focus on the ingredients necessary for the Pasta Machine, which entails a variety of flours, olive oil, and assorted dried spices that I want to flavor the pasta flour with. We need carrot juice (for orange pasta), but finding it in a can is sometimes difficult. Sometimes we have to use a vegetable juice extractor at QVC if we can't find the juice at the market. We also have to make our own spinach juice and beet juice there. And we need bagels for the demonstration on the Pasta Machine, since it comes with a bagel cutter and a bagel knife.

It's now 7:30 P.M, we're finished shopping and now headed to QVC, which is housed in a former pharmaceutical warehouse in the rural town of West Chester. We bring our things into their tiny kitchen, which until recently wasn't much larger than my closet. (They've since remodeled their kitchen and now it's as big as my home kitchen.)

Now comes the fun part: the preparation of the food for the display, all of which I do myself. That means cutting watermelons, cantaloupes, and honeydew melons, and slicing strawberries, tomatoes, mushrooms, apricots, and carrots. I lay out a variety of herbs, spices, fruits, and vegetables in a nice display on thirty-five separate Food Dehydrator trays.

Now I line one of the trays with Saran Wrap and red applesauce to show the customer how to make homemade fruit roll-ups. I lay out soy sauce, brown sugar, and liquid smoke to show how to make jerky. The meat has to be sliced an eighth of an inch thick (the butcher needs to do that for you at the market—and naturally he does it for us.) Apples have to be sliced and put on the tray along with bananas, which can get really tedious. They have to be cut thin and soaked in a lemon-juice solution for the TV cameras, so their colors remain true under the hot lights and don't turn brown.

After preparing all these vegetables and fruits, putting them on the trays, and plugging in six or seven of these machines, we're *almost* ready.

Now it's ten P.M., we still haven't eaten, but we also haven't dealt with all the dried fruits, vegetables, herbs, and spices packaged in the Ziploc bags. These were prepared on the West Coast and need to be taken out of the box and positioned in front of the Food Dehydrators carrying similar foods while they're in operation. Then we have to display the store-bought foods to show the customer the difference between what they buy in the store, such as raisins with chemicals in them, soup mixes loaded with salt, and so on, and what they can do with the machine.

Pasta Time

Now that we're finished with the dehydrator, we have to focus on the Pasta Machine. I normally use six machines, and this is a very tricky situation. In order to maximize the selling time, to get the customers' attention, I want them to see a variety of different shaped and colored pastas coming out—beet rigatoni, spinach fettuccine, carrot angel hair pasta, et cetera.

It probably sounds easy to make that kind of a presentation, but there's one problem: noise from four Pasta Machines working all at the same time.

If the host of the show is selling something else before my appearance, I can't operate the machines because of the sound. So the machines have to be turned on and off, on and off, and if that's not done, you take the chance that the pasta will dry in the dies and then not come through. This presents a unique problem of making sure that I keep the machines operating intermittently, every thirty seconds, just to keep the dies from clogging up.

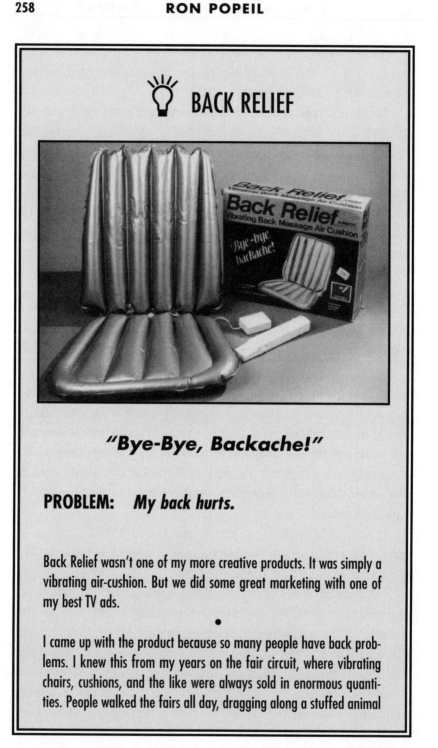

💡 BACK RELIEF

"Bye-Bye, Backache!"

PROBLEM: *My back hurts.*

Back Relief wasn't one of my more creative products. It was simply a vibrating air-cushion. But we did some great marketing with one of my best TV ads.

•

I came up with the product because so many people have back problems. I knew this from my years on the fair circuit, where vibrating chairs, cushions, and the like were always sold in enormous quantities. People walked the fairs all day, dragging along a stuffed animal or two they won at the carnival, and by the time they got to the product booths, they would be so tired. They hadn't sat down all day, so when they rested in a vibrating chair, sales were made instantly. They felt great.

•

Vibrating cushions and chairs have that kind of effect on you if you have a back problem or if you're tired. So why not create one for TV marketing? The market was huge.

•

I knew that vibration helps create circulation, and that's always good where something hurts. So I decided to name this small air-cushion that looked like a seat "Back Relief." It was very inexpensive to make, and you could position the vibration anywhere—wherever the pain hurt you the most.

•

I created a great commercial and an even better name for the product. I mention the name because for those of you reading the book with inventing/marketing ambitions, you really want to stay away from products that have medical connotations. The Federal Trade Commission and the Food and Drug Administration and heavens knows what other organization will come down on you for misleading advertising.

•

It's my understanding that the word *relief* is a safe word to use in marketing products that offer some kind of medical help. Words to definitely stay away from in this category: *cure, eliminates, solves,* or *gets rid of.* But *relief* works.

•

"If you need back relief, or you know someone who needs back relief, give them the perfect Christmas gift and they'll say bye-bye, backache. $24.88. Batteries included."

I'm telling you, it's not as easy as it looks.

Once I have the pasta situation under control, I then need to arrange all the accessories, plus the ingredients the machine is to use—packaging and booklets. And then I'm done. It's midnight, Mike and I still haven't eaten, and I'm going to go on camera in about an hour. But first I have to change my shirt. I'm totally soaked from five hours of preparation.

Wee Hours

When I go to QVC, my first airing is usually twelve-thirty or one A.M., ET. That's when they have a cooking show. Though it's not the best of time slots, it does frequently work. People buy at that hour. But I have to work doubly as hard at one A.M. to get people's attention. At that time of the night every minute is like an hour when people are fighting off the urge to go to sleep. (Speaking of sleep, I began my day at five A.M. PT and now it's getting close to two A.M. ET and I am dead beat.)

Actually, you've got great buyers at one A.M. and two A.M. because they're in a relaxed state of mind, the programming competition is weak, and nobody is bothering them or taking their attention away with phone calls. The kids are asleep. It's very easy for them to see something that catches their fancy, and with a simple phone call, they can be in possession of the product in just a few short days.

Quality timewise, one A.M. is tops. But from a pure dollars-and-cents standpoint, you'd rather be on at twelve noon or seven-thirty P.M. For my July 1994 QVC appearance I sold 625 Pasta Machines at one A.M., which is a pretty hefty number for that hour of the morning. But eleven hours later, when I returned at noon, I moved 2,600 machines.

And to finish the story about my trip to QVC: I went on at one A.M., did fifteen minutes, sold 625 machines (worth

$100,000, not a bad number!), and now comes the real fun: cleaning up the mess I've made during the demonstration! Very little work has to be done with the dehydrators. I can leave them as they were. (The machines are left operating overnight.) But the Pasta Machines all have to be cleaned, washed, and dried. Once that's done, it's two A.M., and we can finally leave and get to Denny's (always open) for some chow.

Then it's a twenty-minute drive to our hotel, some shut-eye, and we're back at QVC the next morning at six A.M. to prepare for my seven A.M. slot. I'll do another one at 12:30 P.M. and then again at seven P.M. Total sales for the July trip: Eight hundred thousand dollars' worth of merchandise. The profit obtained in one twenty-four-hour period was $200,000. Not bad for a day's work. And on top of that we walked away with QVC reorders for 6,500 more Pasta Machines. (Later in September, I devoted a day to the Food Dehydrator and sold 32,000 units in one day.)

Additionally, keep in mind the benefit of roughly forty-five minutes to an hour of free national TV exposure, at no cost to my company. Who knows how many Pasta Machines will sell at retail because of the QVC appearances?

CHAPTER **24**

Retail

There's going to come a time, if you're able to survive the infomercial business, that you're going to want to consider getting into retail. The only way you can achieve big dollars today—because of the high cost of media—is to end up going to retail. Especially if it's a consumer product that solves a problem, rather than a how-to video. Whatever you sell on television, you're going to sell a heck of a lot more in retail stores.

In fact, direct marketing—catalogs, home shopping channels, infomercials, et cetera—account for only some 2.8 percent of the nation's $600-billion-a-year retail marketplace. Let me repeat that, for emphasis: $600 billion!

The retail marketplace is where the big bucks are, and I don't see that ever changing. People like the convenience of buying from TV, but most prefer going to the store and feeling, holding, and really inspecting a product before they decide to buy it. But even were I to make sales in the trillions,

I must confess that, for me, retail is one of the most frustrating businesses there is. I hate it with a passion.

The infomercial business is wonderful when media prices are reasonable, because you're in total control. You decide how you ship the product and where you buy media time. You sell direct to your customers with no middleman in the way. There are no serious collection problems, your customers just keep buying more and more of your products, and you bank more of their money.

Doing business with retailers will drive you crazy, if you're not crazy already. They have *total* power. There's a correlation between a policeman on the beat and the buyer for a retail chain. At the station, dealing with his superiors, the cop is like a little boy. Moving among his street clientele he's a different man.

After selecting your product, buyers for the retail chains are the toughest people you'll ever encounter, and they're interested in only one thing: price. Getting it lower and lower, no matter what price you give them. Their one goal is to squeeze you and squeeze you. They're hard to reach. They usually don't return your phone calls promptly. If you do get a call back, they'll use every method they know of to knock your product down so they can get a better price.

As I've said, the price of media time prevents anyone today from making a fortune in infomercials like we used to back in the early 1990s. But in retail, with the right product and marketing, you can still make millions.

Take my Pasta Machine. Let's say I wanted to sell it to retail (it's currently in retail stores). Say my cost of goods was $50 and I sell it to them for $110. That means I'll make a profit of $60 on each machine. Wal-Mart and Kmart both have about 1,700 stores each, Target has 1,200, the Price Club and Sam's Wholesale Club have roughly 1,000 stores. Figure there are 1,000 Caldor, Macy's, Thrifty, Walgreen, and Woolworth stores. You can go on and on. That's 6,600

💡 THE RONCO GLASS FROSTER

"Enjoy refreshing frosted drinks anywhere"

This was an idea that I conceived of after watching so many beer commercials. Everyone always seemed to be drinking beer out of frosted glasses. The only place you ever got a frosted mug was in a bar, so we set out to find a way for consumers to enjoy them at home. Designer/engineer Herman Brickman came up with the Ronco Glass Froster: by inserting a can of Freon into the plastic holder and giving it a squirt, the consumer would have a frosted glass, instantly.

•

The product came to an end due to the bad publicity about Freon. It was later believed that Freon helped to destroy the ozone layer. So when the federal government passed legislation to remove all Freon from consumer products (except in certain categories, like air-conditioning), the Glass Froster quickly died.

> •
>
> I, by the way, love to drink out of frosted glasses at home, but I do it the old-fashioned way. I put a wet glass into the freezer.
>
> •
>
> *"The gift that will be remembered. Gets parties and dinners off to the right start!"*

stores. Pick any number of Pasta Machines you think any one store could sell in one week. I'm on TV advertising the product every day. How does at least one sound? At Christmas you know they'll sell a hell of a lot more. So that's 52 pieces a year, times 6,600, times my profit of $60. That's $3,120 for the one store, or more than $20 million for the whole chain of stores. On one product. A product with no marketing expense, because the advertising (the infomercial) is paying for itself with orders from TV viewers!

My method before going to retail is to inundate the consumer with millions of dollars in TV advertising time before my product comes to the store so when we call on the buyer, he can say, "Oh, I've seen that on television already. I like it. When can we put it in?"

But I don't make the call.

Because of my past history with retail buyers (I once told one to "get the f*** out of my office" when he tried to strong-arm my price down), I have found that the best way for me to do business is to keep away from them. I just don't speak their language.

Entrepreneurs who develop a product and really believe in it sometimes have a very hard time when they come into contact with a buyer. Yours is just another product out of a thousand to them. They don't feel what you feel. But still, you have to grin and bear it, because they are the ultimate gatekeeper. Whatever they say goes, because they are your outlet to possible wealth.

But at this stage of my career I don't have to bow down to them. Since my personality and wealth allow me to be somewhat independent—and knowing how I react when I get around retail buyers—I instead turn the process over to my trusted associate Mike Srednick, who is much better at dealing with them—and who does speak their language.

Retail Problems

The retail business presents a whole set of problems we should address. And it's not just returned merchandise.

Any substantial retailer who agrees to take your product on will then put your item through quality control. And every store has different standards. Some like the drop test at six feet, others at seven feet. So you may pass, say, Wal-Mart and Kmart, but fail Target, and have to do something about it if you want Target to carry your merchandise.

And then there's advertising. What if you're marketing a product on television for $150, take it to retail, and it starts appearing in their ads for $139.95? You can't tell a retailer what to sell your product for. They could decide to make it a loss leader. Imagine that I'm advertising the Food Dehydrator heavily in Los Angeles at $59.95 and I decide to sell it to the Thrifty chain for $30. Then, to get people in the door, they do a special sale and advertise a special price in the *Los Angeles Times* of $29.95. Now the whole city of L.A. is deader than a doornail for TV.

I didn't sell the Food Dehydrator in retail stores for exactly that reason. I was making too much money off TV and didn't want to hurt that business. But my decision was a costly error.

Here's why: Retail buyers later told me that since they couldn't buy my product, they went to some of my competitors who knocked it off with a cheap version. My decision, I estimate, cost me $50 million in lost sales that instead went to some of my uncreative friends, who took advantage of my advertising with a product that looked like mine.

Every product that's ever been successful on TV has been copied. In fact, there are people out there who focus on nothing but making knockoffs. One guy, who I won't name, always drives me crazy, because whenever I run into him, he always says, "Hey, Ron, why don't you tell me what your next product is so I don't have to wait? I can just knock it off now."

My old commercials have even been knocked off into an infomercial. Mike Levey introduced the "Super Slicer" kitchen gadget in 1994, a cross between the old Dial-O-Matic and Veg-O-Matic. In his infomercial his demonstrator said that the only tears you'd shed while chopping an onion would be "tears of joy," a direct quote from my old 1950s ads.

Was I furious when I saw the infomercial? No. In this business we live in a knockoff society. I wasn't selling the Dial-O-Matic anymore, so he put a new name on an old TV product and put a lot of advertising dollars behind it. That's the nature of this business.

The Clubs

I love selling my products to the clubs—Sam's Wholesale Club, Costco, B.J.'s, the Price Club, and other stores like that. Huge mass market merchandisers who bring people into their warehouses by offering a thin 10 percent markup on goods, less service, and giant aisles.

They also don't advertise specific products, which I love, with the exception of their own mail-order catalog. (That catalog has created, as of this writing, a furor among the top-line department stores who see a product that's similar in packaging and content to some that they stock. They're upset because of the much lower price.)

The clubs have a minimal effect on your TV sales. And for you new inventors/marketers out there, it may be easier for you to break through the door because a heavy TV advertising campaign isn't as important to them as it is to a Kmart or Wal-Mart. All they care about is a quality product at a very low price.

As a television marketer you benefit because they generally don't advertise in newspapers or on TV for specific products. You can also sell more goods to them because they sell more goods, since their prices are very low at retail.

How to Have Your Cake and Eat It Too

But there is a happy medium here. I've figured out a way to sell my product at retail before the knockoffs arrive. It all comes back to upselling.

If you recall, I told you about how we try to sell premium versions of the Food Dehydrator (more trays) and the Pasta Machine (more dies) to our mail order customers for more money than is advertised on TV.

I give those upgraded packages to the retailers at a slightly higher price, to ensure that they won't discount below my TV price. If they do go on sale, they end up selling for around the same price as I offer on TV.

My product is deeply discounted at the clubs, but consumers expect great deals there. That's why they go out of their way to shop at the clubs. They realize you usually have to pay for extra service. The clubs don't affect your TV business. You have to protect the retail price on TV at all costs. Without the infomercial (or commercial) it's hard to get into cable home shopping channels; there's no direct outbound telemarketing by you, no ancillary products, no selling of names, if you don't have any mail order customers.

By offering retailers the premium model and taking a little less profit, everyone hopefully wins.

Buyers

You'll find in dealing with retail buyers that they can be very demanding. Some have become power crazy and you'll have to treat them with kid gloves. We had a situation with a buyer from one of the major discount chains who was furious with us because we had met with the CEO of his firm before we met with him.

But let's say you weren't currently doing business with this chain, and the opportunity to meet with the CEO came up. Wouldn't you do it? Of course you would. Even if you know you're going to be confronted by the buyer later, who is not going to be happy with you.

You have to make him understand that you didn't do it intentionally to make him upset, but the opportunity came up. There's always the chance that the buyer will be so upset he'll either refuse to carry your product (unlikely, since he knows you met with the CEO), or more likely, take only a few pieces and make life hard for you.

It's a trade-off, a catch-22. As a manufacturer or marketer of products it will be difficult for you to get into the retail chains today. They only have so much space, and if you have made a good connection, you should use it. But how do you get in the door without offending the buyer? You could find yourself caught between a rock and a Wal-Mart.

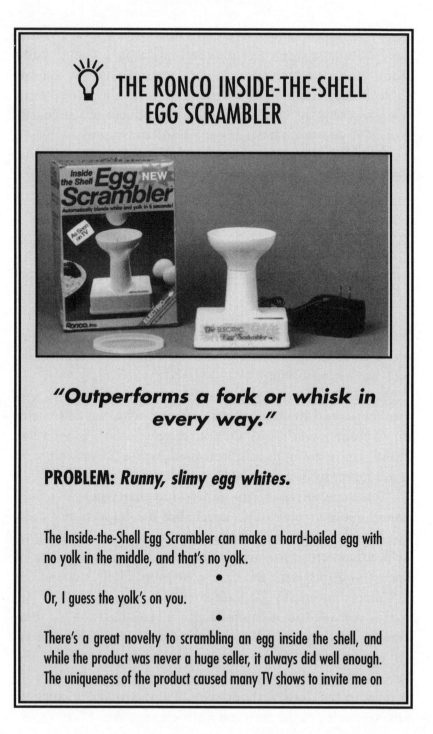

THE RONCO INSIDE-THE-SHELL EGG SCRAMBLER

"Outperforms a fork or whisk in every way."

PROBLEM: *Runny, slimy egg whites.*

The Inside-the-Shell Egg Scrambler can make a hard-boiled egg with no yolk in the middle, and that's no yolk.

•

Or, I guess the yolk's on you.

•

There's a great novelty to scrambling an egg inside the shell, and while the product was never a huge seller, it always did well enough. The uniqueness of the product caused many TV shows to invite me on to talk about my invention. So the Egg Scrambler more than paid for itself with free publicity. (I figure that if you put all my free TV appearances together over the years, and estimate them in dollars, they would add up to over $10 million).

•

The Ronco Inside-the-Shell Egg Scrambler has a curved needle protruding from it. When you impale an egg on the needle, it pushes down on a switch that activates a motor, causing the needle to spin at a very high revolution. The end result being: a perfectly blended egg white and yolk. Now your eggs will look and taste better.

•

I always hated slimy egg whites and knew that I wasn't the only one who felt this way. So I went to my associate, Alan Backus, and we brainstormed on ways to get rid of those slimy whites. We found the answer in Washington, D.C., at the United States Patent Office.

•

Alan looked up old patents and came across a similar product, something that was made in the early 1960s, for a product whose patent had expired. What he found was an egg scrambler that used a needle to solve the problem. You inserted the egg over the needle, and hand-cranked it to scramble the egg. So that gave us a place to start. We used the needle concept and added electricity and other technological updates.

•

The product first came out in the early eighties, and because of popular demand we've just brought it back.

•

"Scrambles the yolk and white of an egg right inside the shell in less than five seconds. You'll use it a lot. And every time you do, you'll save washing a bowl and fork."

Your TV Campaign

Before coming to retail you want to be on TV for at least six months, with a budget that's no less than $150,000 a week. If you don't have that much going for you for six months, you won't create the impact on the consumer and the buyer at the retail store who will purchase your merchandise from you. After you've spent $150,000 a week for six months straight (don't forget, the advertising will bring in sales, which will give you the funds for further TV buys), the consumer will be aware of your product and so will the retail buyer.

Then the decision has to be made after the store has purchased the product from you—how do you proceed with the TV campaign? If you're breaking even or just losing a few dollars, it pays to keep the infomercial running. The second approach is to back up the retail when the product is in stores with short-form one- or two-minute ads. I would also advise that you remove the price from the short-form spots and insert a tag at the end of the commercial, listing the stores in the area where the product can be purchased. But under no circumstance do you tell the retail stores that you will be doing this, because if you do, you'll only get into trouble. They'll probably complain about being bunched in with other stores on the same tag at the end of your commercial.

Trade Shows

What if you have a great product, you've advertised heavily on television, but still can't get in the door to see the big retail buyers? You might want to consider exhibiting at a trade show. These days, there's a convention for everyone (even a beer can collectors' "Canvention"), and the same goes for retail buyers. The hardware show, the housewares show, the Food Marketing Institute, the Consumer Electronics Show (CES)—all these shows specialize in one thing: selling consumer products to retailers. Most conventions have a theme, but increasingly, the lines are blurring as to what constitutes a product for a particular show. The CES, one of the nation's biggest shows, used just to specialize in TVs, radios, and video equipment. But now it's as much a show about computers, telephones, and kitchen gadgets as it is about video.

A trade show is like a living magazine or catalog, where buyers can talk to sellers, see how things work, compare products and prices, and make deals. Most associations *(housewares, hardware, surplus, music merchants, cable TV, water-bed manufacturers)* have one, and they'll be as happy to collect your booth fee money as the next guy. Like a fair, a trade show is very hard work, but every buyer who walks in the door has come there for one reason, and one reason alone—to buy new products for their business.

A big difference between a fair and a trade show is who attends. At a fair you sell directly to the consumer; at a trade show, buyers for stores decide on various products. So your production schedule will be based on orders written at the show or soon thereafter. And all you'll have to bring with you to the show will be a few samples, as opposed to rows and rows of merchandise. Very little actual merchandise changes hands—you're there to take orders for product that will be shipped in the future. Sometimes on the last day of the convention, however, exhibitors will sell their show samples at a deep discount; this way they don't have to ship them back home.

At a convention you will need a much more elaborate booth than you've used at fairs. Conventions are show business, and delegates expect to be dazzled. Competition to stop traffic is much more fierce—you're dealing with real pros on the convention floor—and one way to do it is with an eye-catching booth. Great signage, wild colors, music, a brass band, free popcorn, a beautiful tall woman handing out a flyer to get you to stop. Light, sound, and motion. These are all things that happen on convention floors every day.

Even if you're not exhibiting, there's something to be said for attending a convention before you're ready to start making your product. Conventions are the greatest networking opportunity in the world. If you want to meet a top executive of a major retail chain, you know you'll never get him on the telephone, but he could be at a convention. The program might say that he's a featured speaker, and you could approach him after his speech.

Everyone wears a name tag at conventions, so people are easy to spot. Besides making the big contact, trade shows are just great places to meet other people like yourself; to talk about your common successes and failures, mistakes you all made along the way, and how to avoid them. Most trade shows also feature educational seminars conducted by experts on improving marketing and selling skills, and on the outlook and trends for their industry.

Something else that should be quite obvious: Walking a trade floor is a great way to get new ideas. You see all the new products, displayed in a way that you've never seen in a store, and you can't help but come away with ideas and concepts that will lead to you creating something out of what you've seen.

Just don't expect to walk away an instant millionaire after your first trade show. These things take time. In fact, if it's your first show, expect to exhibit way in the back. The best booth spaces usually go to the leaders of the industry, who pay a price for them, and nab the best locations because of their years in business and sales record.

You'll probably be in a faraway corner with other start-up companies. Traffic will be much lighter. You'll have to work extra hard to attract people to your booth, which will sharpen your sales and marketing skills right away. And once you've gotten a good spot, the same spot is usually offered to you the following year. Unless a company drops out of the show, these great locations are hard to come by.

One last note: Take time, as you would at a fair, to ensure that the convention you've selected is right for your business. Most big conventions are in the big cities—Las Vegas, Chicago, San Francisco, Atlanta, and New Orleans, to name a few—and it takes a considerable amount of effort and money to get there. For instance, besides travel, there are also booth fees, union fees, shipping, hotel accommodations, and food. Ask the trade show organizer the same kinds of hard questions I suggested in the fair section. The most obvious concern of yours: "What kind of buyers do you attract and how many will be there?" My advice to you is, *never go to a first time show!* You may get a great location, but what good is that if nobody attends?

We exhibit the Pasta Machine at conventions dedicated to housewares, gourmet food, and hardware. You may initially scoff at hardware, but most hardware stores today (and that loose term can include everyone from the small True Value shop to the large Home Club) have huge kitchen product sections next to the tools and nails. These are the factors to consider in deciding which show to attend.

Would it make sense to exhibit at a huge convention like the Consumer Electronics Show, even if your product isn't exactly right for it? (Say, a kitchen product for a convention more interested in high tech.) All you need is an electrical product, and if a space is still available, you're in. A lot of big conventions are categorizing in specific locations—for instance, all the electrical or kitchen appliance firms in one specific area of the convention floor.

The CES attracts 100,000 people, and competition for

buyers is fierce. But even if you reached only (!) 500 buyers, it might not be a bad place to begin with.

On the other hand, if you brought your kitchen product to the housewares show in Chicago, which has a much smaller crowd (50,000), your chances of breaking through to the buyers would be much easier. It just depends on how hard it would be for you to get to either of these conventions. For the CES, maybe you live in Los Angeles and can drive to Las Vegas and stay over with some friends. Then maybe it would be worth it.

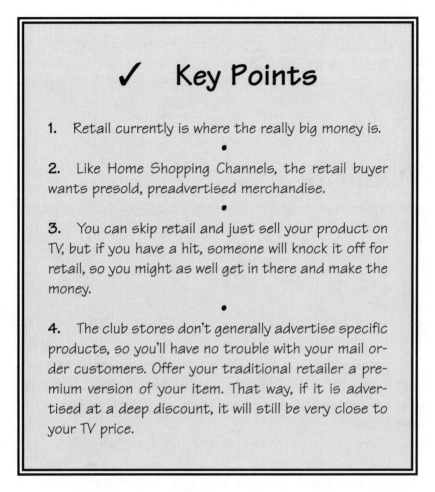

✓　Key Points

1.　Retail currently is where the really big money is.

•

2.　Like Home Shopping Channels, the retail buyer wants presold, preadvertised merchandise.

•

3.　You can skip retail and just sell your product on TV, but if you have a hit, someone will knock it off for retail, so you might as well get in there and make the money.

•

4.　The club stores don't generally advertise specific products, so you'll have no trouble with your mail order customers. Offer your traditional retailer a premium version of your item. That way, if it is advertised at a deep discount, it will still be very close to your TV price.

CHAPTER **2 5**

Publicity

The media love inventors. We're an alternate celebrity to an actor or actress pushing their latest film. Instead, we push our new products, and we get so much in return for our appearances.

We're also grist for the parody mill. Dan Aykroyd used to go after me on *Saturday Night Live* with the "Bass-O-Matic" (a blender that ground, chopped, diced, and sliced fish) and recently Danny DeVito played Ron Popeil himself in a spoof of my GLH commercial. Homer gave Bart a Mr. Microphone type product on *The Simpsons,* and my products have been mentioned in movies ranging from *Sneakers* to *Wayne's World II.*

One night I was home watching *Jeopardy!* and got a pleasant surprise: one category was devoted to Ronco products. And I did get all the answers right, Alex, for a change.

Anytime you can get on free media to sell yourself and your company: *Do it.* I've been on so many TV shows (invariably interviewed on my porch in front of rows and rows

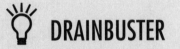 **DRAINBUSTER**

"Strong power for blockage of drains"

PROBLEM: *Clogged plumbing pipes.*

After I came out of semiretirement in 1991 with the Ronco Electric Food Dehydrator, we opened the *Incredible Inventions* infomercial by having me show off several of my new and old products before we started talking about the Food Dehydrator.

•

I began by talking about the Drainbuster, a nineties-style plunger. The difference was that it uses air to clear your plumbing pipes in syringe fashion.

•

Drainbuster was brought to me by a company in the Orient. I never really got involved with the product seriously, and dropped it midstream, because I realized there was too much competition in the foreign marketplace with similar products. I was unaware of that when I initially got involved. My concern was that I didn't want to deal with foreign competition coming over here and undercutting me after I spent millions of dollars advertising on TV.

•

When I talked about the Drainbuster in the dehydrator infomercial, I explained how it worked and said I hadn't marketed it yet. I never did.

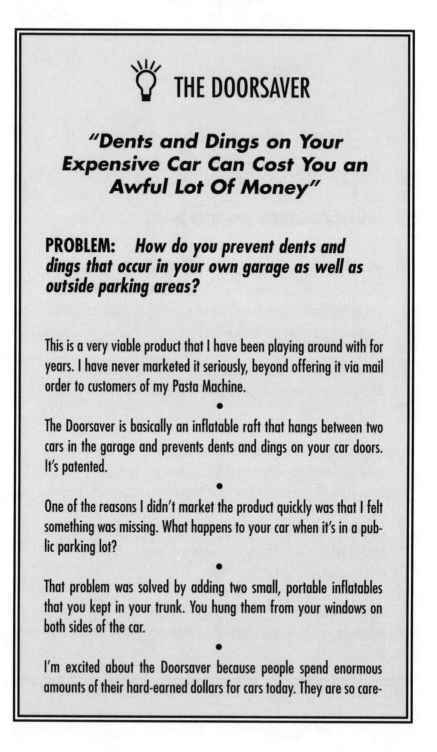

THE DOORSAVER

"Dents and Dings on Your Expensive Car Can Cost You an Awful Lot Of Money"

PROBLEM: *How do you prevent dents and dings that occur in your own garage as well as outside parking areas?*

This is a very viable product that I have been playing around with for years. I have never marketed it seriously, beyond offering it via mail order to customers of my Pasta Machine.

•

The Doorsaver is basically an inflatable raft that hangs between two cars in the garage and prevents dents and dings on your car doors. It's patented.

•

One of the reasons I didn't market the product quickly was that I felt something was missing. What happens to your car when it's in a public parking lot?

•

That problem was solved by adding two small, portable inflatables that you kept in your trunk. You hung them from your windows on both sides of the car.

•

I'm excited about the Doorsaver because people spend enormous amounts of their hard-earned dollars for cars today. They are so care-

---

ful about the looks of their second largest investment. There's a great market potential here. By the time you're reading this book, the Ronco Doorsaver commercial should be on the airwaves, and the product will be available via television or at a store near you.

---

of past and present Ronco or Popeil products). I do two or three radio interviews a week. I've been profiled in all the leading newspapers. And every time, sales go up.

Always throw out your 800 number whenever you can, even if they try to block it. I once did the *Late Night with Conan O'Brien* and yelled out 1-800-43-RONCO, but NBC bleeped out the last 25 percent. (I guess they didn't want to give me a free ad.) I also did *NBC Nightly News* with Tom Brokaw, and when they showed a clip of my infomercial, they covered the last digit of my toll-free number. But that didn't stop 1,250 orders the next day from people who used their brain and guessed the right number.

I had no intention of going on the show and deriving any direct financial benefit from it, but the money flowed in anyhow, and that's just another reward of publicity. I figure my Tom Brokaw appearance was worth about $42,500. At least that's how much merchandise we sold the next day. Who knows how it affected sales over the next weeks?

Unlike most companies, I don't employ publicity agents. They call me!

Is it hard to get booked on the shows? Not if you have an interesting, unique product. Local news programs and talk shows are always looking for what's hot and new, and they love local angles. That's what differentiates them from network TV and gives locals a reason to watch.

The same rules apply to the print media. What's wrong

with calling your local newspaper, asking for the business section, and telling them about your amazing new product? Nothing. This could be the beginning of the great publicity snowball.

USA Today was doing a story on men's hair products, and they called my assistant Gina asking for some samples. She put the package together and came to me for my approval. I didn't want to send them. And I called the reporter, Arlene Vigoda, to explain why.

"Arlene, if you test my product, and I can't stop you from doing that, how do you know that I won't do something to the product to make it more enhanceable than it really is?" I said. "I don't send product out for testing. Most of the people who test, I have no idea how they test. Every time I tell people how to use GLH, I say to hold it a couple of inches away. Yet on every TV show I've ever been on, they always hold it ten or twelve inches away, and of course, the spray gets much wider and gets all over everything.

"So, Arlene, here's what I want to do. I'll come to you. I'll show you how it's used. I'll demonstrate it for your editors. And then you can demonstrate it for anybody else after I've left."

Arlene's editors approved my visit, and now I'm on a plane for Washington, D.C. I go to the *USA Today* offices in Arlington, Virginia, and everybody there seems to know me. They've used one of my products at some point in their lives and want to talk about it. I demonstrate GLH to several of the reporters and editors and they freak out. Naturally, I've won them over. What at first was just going to be a product test had blossomed into something much bigger.

So when the article came out, there was no mention of competing hair products. In fact, the final product turned out to be a front page "Life" section profile of Ron Popeil, his life, background, and products. It was almost a full page of Ron Popeil. Just because I got into the driver's seat.

In the publicity business one thing leads to another. Other journalists saw the *USA Today* article, and the phone started ringing off the hook. The *Chicago Tribune. 20/20. Prime-Time Live. The Maury Povich Show. The Washington Post.* It started to pyramid, all because I made the right decision not just to send some free cans of GLH in the mail. I got off my ass and did it the right way. And my world changed because of it.

Newspaper exposure is great because it translates into future TV bookings. And one thing to remember about getting on TV is that if you go out seeking TV exposure, the person in charge—the "booker"—will ask for "tape."

Translated, that means you'll need to send video of your prior appearances, so that the producers of the show can get some idea of how you look on camera. They want to see that you're witty, snappy, good-looking, and entertaining.

So be sure to videotape all of your appearances, no matter how minor. Because not only can you use them for future bookings, they're also an important sales tool at fairs and trade shows. You can stick a TV monitor at your booth, and play, over and over again, your reel of prior TV appearances. Fairgoers will get a kick out of seeing you demonstrating your product in front of a celebrity and an audience, and it's just another sales tool to get them to buy.

Also, in your infomercial, you might want to use a clip from your prior TV appearance. The show might say no, because they don't want their show used in the infomercial format. But you'll never know if you don't ask. And you might have a better chance of getting the permission if you go to them with only one request. Why bog them down by asking them to dig your clip out of the library as well?

CHAPTER **26**

And Finally . . .

Confidence

I'm very proud of the products I sell today. I totally believe in my products, and can sell anything I believe in.

Even if you're not a good public speaker and you're worried about being nervous demonstrating your product on TV—don't be! If you really believe in your product, know it works, and have the confidence that you can make it a success, you'll have no problem once the camera turns your way.

It's you and the product speaking.

In most TV appearances there's not enough time to be nervous. There are no endless bouts of chitchat between you and the host or hostess before launching into your demo. With the time constraints of today you're given seven or eight minutes, most of which is tied up with you showing off your product. The experience is really no different from doing it in your own home. By the time you get through telling your story and the benefits of your product that you've lived through from the first day of development through the advertising, you don't have time to get nervous.

Besides, I can tell you right now what kind of questions you're going to be asked, so start practicing your snappy short answers, or "sound bites." Your bites should be no longer than a sentence or two.

1. *How did you get started inventing?*
2. *How did you invent this product?*
3. *Does it really work?*
4. *What's next for you?*

Could I Sell Anything?

Several interviewers over the years have referred to me as the master salesman, a guy who could sell you anything, but I don't agree. Could I sell real estate? Yes, if I believed in a house. But I don't really feel that all the homes real estate agents sell to their customers are in the best interests of their customers. You have to understand your buyers and what their objectives are. It's a lot different from the Pasta Machine, where every unit is the same. You know every nook and cranny, how it works, how it performs, and how the consumer will enjoy it.

Many successful people today sold things early in their careers that later in life they wouldn't sell. They matured, learned from their mistakes, and progressed to things they really would have liked to start out with.

So do I have a questionable past? Not really. But I do look back at some of my old products, and today, I wouldn't go near them with a ten-foot pole. The products weren't meaningful; it was my marketing that sold them. Those mistakes in learning have elevated me to a place in my life where

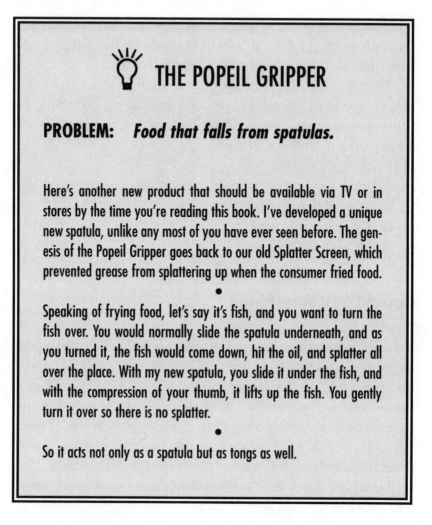

THE POPEIL GRIPPER

PROBLEM: *Food that falls from spatulas.*

Here's another new product that should be available via TV or in stores by the time you're reading this book. I've developed a unique new spatula, unlike any most of you have ever seen before. The genesis of the Popeil Gripper goes back to our old Splatter Screen, which prevented grease from splattering up when the consumer fried food.

•

Speaking of frying food, let's say it's fish, and you want to turn the fish over. You would normally slide the spatula underneath, and as you turned it, the fish would come down, hit the oil, and splatter all over the place. With my new spatula, you slide it under the fish, and with the compression of your thumb, it lifts up the fish. You gently turn it over so there is no splatter.

•

So it acts not only as a spatula but as tongs as well.

quality is paramount. It's easy to make those kinds of bad decisions when you're young and struggling to create wealth.

If I could pass on something to my reader, I'd love it to be this: Don't make the same mistake I did. Try, if possible, to make quality your first priority. Sometimes quality costs you more to produce, but the rewards are much greater.

My Success

So, was I a genius? The greatest inventor of all time? A brilliant strategist? Not at all. I think I was just lucky enough to be in the right place at the right time. Once I got through the pain of growing up, from my late teens on I always felt myself to be incredibly lucky and have great timing.

I got involved with TV when it was new—who knew it would be so big? That was luck. Steve Wynn having an opening on the Golden Nugget (now Mirage Resorts) board of directors when I happened to be in Las Vegas one day—luck again. Selling $100 million worth of my Food Dehydrator— something that had been around for ten years—through the new medium of infomercials. Again, great timing, great luck. Being in the right place at the right time.

Even a product like the Inside the Outside Window Washer, which didn't make me any real money and which I consider a flop—well, I didn't lose any money. And I gained a whole lot of experience.

Is There a Product I Wish I Had Invented?

My number one question on TV talk shows: *What product do I wish I had invented?* My answer: the Clapper. A lot of people thought it was mine, but it wasn't. I had nothing to do with it. However, I'm disappointed I didn't come up with the great idea of a device that turned off lights, stereo, and the TV just by clapping your hands.

The product was simple, entertaining, and it solved a problem. How many times did you want to turn off a light switch or the TV, yet you don't want to get up to do it? That's a very common occurrence. In fact, it happened to me the other night.

So why didn't I just clap them off? Because I don't own the Clapper. And why not? I guess I'm a little jealous. It would keep reminding me of something I should have made.

The Line I Want on My Tombstone

The knife I'm demonstrating is so sharp, it will even cut a cow. And that's no bull.

Actually, my tombstone will have to be very large. I think people perceive me as a very successful marketer and inventor of products, but what they really remember is that I was a part of their lives in their bedroom, living room, anywhere they had a TV set.

It was my voice, my face, my hands, and it always ended in "And it's only four easy payments of $39.95" or "Still just $2.98 and it makes a perfect gift!"

Ron Popeil was a man who you weren't married to, in fact never met, but who was a part of your family. You grew up with me and my products and everybody has their favorites, whether it's the Pocket Fisherman, Mr. Microphone, or Chop-O-Matic. People ask me all the time to name a favorite, but I can't. That's like having to name your favorite child. I will say that I thought the ad we did for Mr. Microphone was our best, because it was so entertaining, and that I received more positive feedback about the Pasta Machine than any other product I ever invented or marketed. But as far as a favorite, or my all-time best product, that's in the future, because my mind doesn't go backward, but forward to the next one.

The Stars of Infomercials

Of all of the people who have become stars in the infomercial business, I think motivational speaker and author Anthony Robbins is the best at what he does. He has charisma and a speaking quality that causes the consumer to pay attention. Weight-loss maven Susan Powter, who's often called the Queen of Infomercials to Ron Popeil's "King" status, is very credible in areas that she believes in. And she certainly knows how to get attention.

Mike Levey has done a great job of taking the fair pitch to TV. He capitalized on the infomercial business by associating himself with pitchmen from the foreign marketplace to introduce products here. Most of his products and presentations originated at fairs.

Victoria Principal, Dionne Warwick, Ali MacGraw, Cher—they're just celebrities putting their name to a product. Is the consumer led to believe that this is the creation of the celebrity, or just a paid endorsement? Many celebrities will accept remuneration and basically say anything to sell you the product. I believe you shouldn't have to pay for endorsements. Let the product speak for itself.

Anthony Robbins is a very powerful salesman and speaker. I believe he could sell anything. I do know, however, that he doesn't watch TV. How am I so sure? We were both at the NIMA (National Infomercial Marketing Association) trade show in Las Vegas in 1993. I was walking down an aisle, and most people there knew who I was because of my years in the industry and all the money I've spent on TV advertising over the years. I was also a featured speaker at the show.

Anyway, who do I see coming toward me, but Anthony Robbins. I had never met him but always admired his abilities. We walked up to each other and I held out my hand to shake his. "Hi, Tony, I'm Ron Popeil."

"Hi, Ron . . . and what do you do for a living?"

When I flew back to Los Angeles, most of the people on the plane had come from the NIMA convention, and everybody was talking about how Anthony Robbins had never heard of Ron Popeil. "What does this guy do during the night?" one guy behind me said. "He certainly doesn't watch TV."

What I Watch on TV

What does a guy who's made millions from the TV set watch on TV? Not much. I occasionally tune in to *60 Minutes* and *20/20,* but the rest of the time, it's strictly commercials. Where other people are flicking through the commercials to seek better programming, I'm studying my competition. I'm watching for cleverness, the quality of camera work, lighting, and close-ups, especially when it comes to products related to food.

You can never stop learning and picking up tips. I have a dozen TV sets all over my house, all with VCRs attached, and always attempt to catch various products that I know will be aired.

What I don't watch are my competitors' infomercials. Knowing that most of them are scripted and acted out takes away, I believe, from the credibility of the show and possibly the product. Mine are ad-libbed and true. I take pride in that.

I also feel that some of the products being sold on infomercials today are really not as good as they appear, and that hurts my business. Take the "Smart Mop," which in 1994 was one of the big infomercials. This was the mop that supposedly picked up anything better than any other mop ever had done before. I'm sure the mop's fine, but I saw a similar mop demonstration—but not the same price point— back at the fairs forty years ago.

I'm confident the Smart Mop performs, but the emphasis is more on the pitch and pitchman than the product's quality. That's the difference between me and them. I recognize it because I grew up with it in my early business years.

I believe that many of the products sold on infomercials are overpriced. (I'm sure some readers are thinking, *Aha, Popeil's products are overpriced too.* I can't stop people from thinking that.) I believe the BluBlocker sunglasses are overpriced because I can compare them to hundreds of other sunglasses in the marketplace. A great product, I use them, but I still think they're overpriced. When I came out with my Pasta Machine and Food Dehydrator, I undersold my competition.

This industry has certainly rewarded me financially, and made me a celebrity, but I'm concerned that most infomercials today are more focused on the pitch than the product, and that reflects badly on those of us who try to bring out quality products.

Now that the infomercial business has grown up, it's getting harder and harder to find the right product to sell via the medium. The costs of media dictate that the kinds of knickknacks I sold in the sixties and seventies are too hard to sell now, so many have to turn to gimmicky products. Hence, the Smart Mop.

Visibility

A great deal of my success has to do with luck. I selected a business that caused me to go on television, where I didn't have to count on other people to spend their money to give me the visibility that I received. Being able to foot the bill to perpetuate my own visibility in the marketplace has elevated me to some sort of celebrity status.

It's a unique position to have fallen into. I doubt very

much if I could have achieved the kind of success I have to-day if I were in another business. If I had just invented and marketed products and sold them to other people and they used their name on the products—where would I be today?

Had it been the Sam Rosen Automatic Pasta Maker, then Sam Rosen would have gotten all the publicity and hype, even though it was my invention. I would have been suc-cessful in selling him the product, but I wouldn't have re-ceived the acclaim, and the additional money that went along with it.

With visibility I've been able to get huge companies like Fingerhut and General Mills to be associated with me and put my face on TV at their expense. The exposure has cer-tainly paid off for them and for me and my company.

Work for Yourself

I would like to leave you now with my best three words of advice: *Work for yourself.*

People, particularly those in the sales profession, ask me for career tips all the time. Salespeople usually say something like "I'm great in sales, Ron, but not in your league yet. How can I get there?"

By not working for anyone but yourself. If you're a good salesperson, you can make more money in one month selling a product that you make or market than you can in a year working for an employer.

Find that product and get out on the fair circuit. Go to the library and read *Amusement Business.* Check out the list of upcoming fairs and book yourself space to sell. Again, you could easily make over $100,000 a year working weekends on the fair circuit. The hours are long, but there's lots of money to be made and you are your own boss.

I've tried in this book to give you honest, truthful advice.

It worked for me, there's no reason it can't work for you. A fair in the 1950s is no different from a fair in the 1990s. Admission prices have gone up, but the Ferris wheel still goes round and round, the 4-H club shows off livestock, guys like me come to sell their homegrown products, and hundreds of thousands bring their families to shop and have a great time.

If you think you're a good inventor or salesperson, and you've got a good product, you can start with relatively few dollars and pyramid it. Be the next Ron Popeil. Have a quality product, believe in it thoroughly, and go out and sell it.

And don't forget: Make sure it's a great gift.

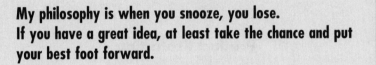

**My philosophy is when you snooze, you lose.
If you have a great idea, at least take the chance and put your best foot forward.**

Resource Guide

Product Protection

The Underwriters Laboratories: 1655 Scott Boulevard, Santa Clara, CA 95050. Telephone: 408-985-2400.

Publications

Amusement Business, P.O. Box 24970, Nashville, TN, 37202. Telephone: 800-999-3322.

Advertising Age, 740 Rush Street, Chicago, IL 60611-2590. Telephone: 312-649-5200.

Electronic Retailing, 7628 Densmore Avenue, Van Nuys, CA 91406. Telephone: 818-782-7328.

Response TV, 201 E. Sandpointe Avenue, Santa Ana, CA 92707-5761. Telephone: 800-854-3112.

Steven Dworman's Infomercial Marketing Report, 11533 Thurston Circle, Los Angeles, CA, 90049. Telephone: 310-472-5253.

Successful Meetings Magazine (for list of upcoming trade shows), Directory Dept., 633 Third Avenue, New York, NY 10017.

Home Shopping Channels

QVC, 1365 Enterprise Drive, West Chester, PA 19380. Telephone: 800-345-1515.

The Home Shopping Network, 11831 30th Ct. North, St. Petersburg, FL 33716. Telephone: 813-572-8585.

Infomercial Trade Association:

The National Infomercial Marketing Assn. (NIMA), 1201 New York Avenue, NW, Suite 1000, Washington, D.C., 20005-3917. Telephone: 800-962-9796; 202-962-8342.

Government Resources

AGENCIES AND PUBLICATIONS

Write to the following agencies for information about their publications and/or services.

Copyright Office, Library of Congress, Washington, D.C. 20559

Circular R 1, Copyright Basics

Circular R 15a, Duration of Copyright

Department of Commerce, Washington, D.C., 20234

Business Services Bulletins

Department of Energy, Assistant General Counsel for Patents, Washington, D.C., 20585

You and the Patenting Process

Small Business Guide to Federal Research and Development Funding Opportunities

Patent and Trademark Office, Washington, D.C. 20231. Telephone: 703-557-3158

Directory of Registered Patent Attorneys and Agents Arranged by States and Counties

General Information Concerning Patents

General Information Concerning Trademarks

Guide for Patent Draftsmen

Index of Patents Issued from the United States Patent and Trademark Office

Index of Trademarks Issued from the United States Patent and Trademark Office

Official Gazette of the United States Patent and Trademark Office
Patent and Trademark Office Notices
Patent Profiles
Patents and Government Developed Inventions
Patents and Inventions: An Informal Aid for Inventors
Questions and Answer About Patents
(To order any of the brochures through the mail, send a check for $2.25 each to the Government Printing Office, Washington, D.C. 20402. Telephone: 202-512-1800. For recorded information about obtaining a patent, call the Patent and Trademark Office's automated information system at 703-557-4636.)
Small Business Administration, P.O. Box 30, Denver, CO 80210-0030. Telephone: 800-368-5855.
Small Business Bibliographies
No. 9, *Marketing Research Procedures*
No. 12, *Statistics and Maps for National Market Analysis*
No. 13, *National Directories for Use in Marketing*
No. 39, *Decision Points in Developing New Products*
No. 89, *Marketing for Small Business*
No. 90, *New Product Development*
No. 91, *Ideas into Dollars: A Resource Guide for Inventors and Innovative Small Businesses.*
Small Business Innovation Research Programs, SBSA Office of Innovation Research and Technology, 1441 First Street, NW, Washington, D.C. 20416.
No. 2.013, *Can You Make Money with Your Idea or Invention?*
No. 4.019, *Learning About Your Market*
No. 2.006, *Finding a New Product for Your Company*
No. 6.005, *Introduction to Patents*

Fullfillment Centers

USA 800 Inc., 6616 Raytown Road, Kansas City, MO 64133. Telephone: 800-821-7539.
Tylie Jones and Associates, 3519 West Pacific Avenue, Burbank, CA 91505. Telephone: 800-922-0662.
PCS Inc., 6211 S. 380 West, Salt Lake City, UT 84107. Telephone: 801-265-9393.

Media Buying

Williams Television Time, 3130 Wilshire Boulevard, Santa Monica, CA 90403. Telephone: 310-828-8600.

American Television Time, 178 Barsana Avenue, Austin, TX 78737. Telephone: 512-288-6400.

Telephone Call Processing

West Telemarketing Corp., 9910 Maple Street, Omaha, NE 68134. Telephone: 800-542-1000.

Telenational Marketing, 7300 Woolworth Avenue, Omaha, NE 68124. Telephone: 800-333-6106.

USA 800 Inc., 6616 Raytown Road, Kansas City, MO 64133. Telephone: 800-821-7539.

Payment Processing and Verification

Charter Pacific Bank, 30141 Agoura Road, Agoura Hills, CA 91301. Telephone: 818-991-8512.

Litle and Company, 54 Stiles Road, Salem, NH 03079. Telephone: 603-893-9333.

Index